The Complete Guide to

Planning
& Managing
Software Projects

How to Finish Projects
On Time and On Budget

Carl Breunlin

SOFTWARE ARCHITECTS, INC.

A Software Architects, Inc., Publication

Chicago, Indianapolis, Tampa, Columbus,
Cincinnati, Dallas, Houston, Phoenix, Denver

ISBN 0-9753715-2-5
LCCN 2004092343

ATTENTION CORPORATIONS, UNIVERSITIES, COLLEGES, AND
PROFESSIONAL ORGANIZATIONS: Quantity discounts are available on
bulk purchases of this book for educational, gift purposes, or as premiums for
increasing magazine subscriptions or renewals. Special books or book excerpts
can also be created to fit specific needs. For information, please contact
Software Architects, Inc., 4 Westbrook Corporate Center, #800,
Westchester, IL 60154; 708-531-5000; *www.sark.com.*

First printing 2004
Manufactured in the United States of America

Dedication

To my Mom and Dad,
who encouraged me to pursue my dreams,
and who, through their total and selfless sacrifices, made
sure I had the tools I needed to pursue those dreams.

Acknowledgments

I would especially like to thank the management team of Software Architects, Inc., for making this book possible. Specifically, I want to thank: Gene Petrie, Ed Wroble, Mark Jensen, and Mike Collins.

Also, a very special thanks to Mitch Rhinehart, who despite his hectic schedule, still made time to help me with the manuscript. Thanks, Mitch.

Also, a special thanks to Kelley Smith, Jennifer Steele, and Jennifer Gardner for helping with the manuscript, figures, and tables.

Thanks also to Nusret Agovic, a talented photographer and good friend, for his photographic contributions used in the design and production of the front cover.

And finally, a very special thanks to my wife Helen, who read, reread, and read again this book from its first inception as a series of articles to the final edited copy. Without her help and support this book would never have been possible.

Thanks again!

About the Author

Carl Breunlin is an expert on IT Project Management. He has twenty-four years of experience managing a variety of software development projects, including real time systems, electronic commerce systems, international web site development, and Business-to-Business (B2B) systems varying in size from those consisting of several software developers to extensive $100 million development efforts.

His vast experience working in a variety of industries has given him unique insight into the needs of real-world managers and developers. His expertise has allowed him to successfully consult with many well-known Fortune 500 companies, providing technical guidance on projects as well as helping develop world-class software development organizations.

He has taught college-level Computer Science courses, including System Design, System Analysis, C++, C and Management Information Systems courses.

Carl is currently the Director of the Project Office for Software Architects, Inc., a full-service, nationally based, software-consulting firm. His primary responsibilities include implementing world-class Project Management practices for Software Architects, Inc. and their clients.

Carl has written over sixty articles on software development. He has also written numerous technical and training manuals.

About Software Architects, Inc.

Software Architects, Inc. is a full-service, nationally based IT solutions provider. Since 1978, the company has implemented systems for some of the country's top companies, working in-step with them to help meet their long-term strategic business goals. The company specializes in custom application development and application integration and prides itself on employing experts in leading-edge technologies.

Software Architects' success in meeting its clients' needs is evidenced by the fact that a majority of its revenues come from repeat business.

Companies continue to turn to Software Architects to develop scalable, reliable, maintainable solutions that meet their business needs. The employees of Software Architects possess proven skills in Project Management, vast experience and knowledge of leading-edge technologies, unrivaled expertise in software architecture, and a proven ability to define business requirements.

Software Architects employs certified professionals and deploys consultant teams throughout the country that consistently demonstrate the highest degree of professionalism and take pride in quality customer service. The company has been recognized by industry leaders and continues to make strides in the world of Information Technology.

For more information on Software Architects, please visit www.sark.com.

Table of Contents

Part 2: Managing the Project, 133

Chapter 8 Managing Cost and Schedule, 135

Chapter 9 Managing Change, 155

Chapter 10 Managing Quality, 171

Chapter 11 Testing, 199

Glossary, 223

Index, 225

Introduction

ONE OF THE BIGGEST problems associated with any new software project is creating an accurate estimate of how much it is going to cost to complete the project. A second problem is converting that estimate into a manageable financial plan that is easy to understand.

The purpose of this book is to provide a comprehensive approach to solving both of these problems. In this book you will find a simple way to estimate and manage software projects. This methodology provides you with a step-by-step roadmap for creating accurate project estimates and converting those estimates into financial project plans from which projects can be managed.

The methodology discussed in this book will show you how to tie the project's cost estimate directly to what has to be built. It will then show you how to convert the estimate into the number of architects, developers, and testers required to complete the project and how to determine when those personnel are required.

Once you know how many resources (architects, developers, etc.) are required and when they are needed, you will learn how to create a budget to support the development staff. You will also learn how to determine the optimum development organization and how to allocate the budget to each part of the organization.

After the organization has been determined and a budget allocated, you will learn how to manage your project according to the budget and schedule.

A key aspect of this methodology is that everything ties directly together. The estimate ties directly to what has to be developed. The number of resources assigned to the project ties directly to the estimate, and the budget ties directly to the resources. Finally, the tools used to manage the project are tied directly to the budget and schedule.

This book was written for everyone involved with a new project, from developers to executives. Developers benefit from the material covered here in that they will learn how to estimate their efforts accurately. Better estimates mean a better chance of completing each part of the project when it is promised.

Project managers benefit by learning how to create accurate financial project plans and how to manage according to those plans. The techniques presented in the following chapters will help project managers of all skill levels be more successful at completing projects on time and on budget.

And finally, executives will benefit by having an approach that accurately answers two pressing questions: "Is the project estimate accurate, and can the project be managed according to the estimate?"

This book is designed to be read from cover to cover. Approached in that manner, the book will provide a comprehensive set of fully integrated tools for estimating and managing projects. Reading the book from cover to cover is the recommended approach.

If you have an extensive background in Project Management, you can also use the book as a reference. For example, if you need information on managing the cost and schedule for a project, turn directly to the chapter on this subject for important insight.

Regardless of the reader's needs and approach, every chapter has been written to be easily read and understood. The book is written for busy people who want answers and want those answers quickly. You will not find academic jargon or vague theories here — just a concrete, easy-to-follow methodology designed to help you complete your projects on time and on budget.

The proven methodology explained in this book will significantly help you to plan and manage your next project.

PART 1

Planning the Project

PART 1 OF THIS BOOK focuses on planning a new software project. In the following chapters you will learn how to:

❑ Estimate the cost, in hours, of the project

❑ Create the budget for the project

❑ Determine, on a monthly basis, what the planned expenditure rate is

❑ Allocate the budget to the development organization

❑ Determine how many people are needed on the project

❑ Determine when those people are needed

In Part 2 of this book, you will learn how to manage your project based on the financial project plan created above.

CHAPTER 1

Getting Started

BEFORE SENIOR MANAGERS approve a new software development project they want to know the answer to two important questions. First, "Is the estimate for the project accurate?" and second, "Can the project be managed according to the estimate?"

Managers are under great pressure to cut cost and live within budgets. Everyone knows that large software projects have the potential to impact corporate budgets adversely if not delivered on time. This is why the initial project estimate is so important. If the original estimate is not correct, the project will likely end up costing more than is expected.

Even if the project is estimated correctly, execution of the project plan must be in accordance with the original estimate. If the project starts deviating from the original plan, there is a significant probability that the project will come in over budget and behind schedule. This is why the answer to the second question is as equally important as the first. If the project manager cannot manage the project according to the original plan, there will likely be significant cost and schedule overruns in the future.

This book will show you how to create an accurate estimate for a project, and it will also show you how to manage the project according to that estimate. Knowing how to estimate a project's cost and schedule accurately and how to manage according to those estimates are keys to completing any project on time and on budget.

The material in this book has been written on the assumption that the reader and his team have the technical skills required to build a software system, so this book does not cover design and coding issues. However, there are some technical aspects of planning and managing that are very important to creating accurate estimates — for example, collecting system requirements. Without a good set of requirements, it is impossible to estimate how much a project is going to cost, and it is also impossible to give a good estimate of the completion date. Since requirements are so critical to the project's cost and schedule estimate, we will spend some time learning how to collect them efficiently.

The Importance of an Accurate Estimate

When an organization commits to a major development effort, the executives involved sign up to incur the associated expenses. By agreeing to start a new project, these executives are also forgoing other projects that might be equally important. Making decisions about how to spend limited resources is always difficult. This is why executives want to know exactly how much it is going to cost and when it is going to be finished. Knowing the answer to these questions makes forward planning easier. Executives know how much budget is required in the coming quarters to finish the effort, and they know when the project will be completed. This information lets them know when resources will be available to begin the next important project.

Likewise, when an organization commits to a new software project, the business units that will eventually use the new system expect it to be done when promised. Business units also forward plan and want to know when the new system will be useable. In some cases, the need dates are extremely critical, as with automating new state or federal legislation. In other instances, key competitive advantages are at stake if a new system does not come on line when promised.

In each case, the key point is that completing a project on time and on budget is only meaningful when compared with the originally promised cost and schedule. Because of this, the initial estimate is very critical. It is the original cost and schedule estimate that provide the markers by which cost and schedule fidelity are measured.

What is Involved in Making an Accurate Estimate?

Since the initial estimate is so important, accurately identifying all the factors and tasks that have to be estimated becomes critical. Obviously, a big part of the estimate revolves around estimating the cost of completing development tasks.

This part of the estimate includes the time to gather requirements, design the system, code it, and, of course, test it. These are all important components of a good cost estimate, but in many cases they do not cover all the cost drivers.

Project estimators must also estimate non-developmental tasks such as procuring new hardware. A list of these non-developmental tasks might be quite extensive on some projects and include tasks such as:

❏ Project Management

❏ Configuration Management

❏ Quality Assurance

❏ Meetings

❏ Reporting

❏ Reviews

❏ Test

❑ Training

❑ Etc.

Every project is different, and every project will have a different set of cost drivers. As you will see in Chapter 2, "Executive Planning," these cost drivers are collected in a document called a Statement of Work. The Statement of Work is a key planning document created at the beginning of the estimating process. It contains a list of every task, both developmental and non-developmental, that must be estimated prior to the start of the project.

Creating a Financial Project Plan and Managing the Project

Once a project estimate is complete, it must be converted to a financial project plan. Simply determining that a project is going to cost $3 million to finish is only part of the story. That $3 million must be converted into an equivalent number of people who will do the work and also into an associated schedule. The number of people required to complete the project and the schedule for them to complete their development tasks forms the basis of the financial project plan. Additionally, the financial project plan shows the expected monthly expenditures for the project.

Creating a financial project plan is not enough either. It is one thing to take the original estimate and convert it to a financial project plan and another matter to manage the effort according to the plan. This book will show you how to do that by explaining how to load the financial project plan into a Cost and Schedule Control System (CSCS).

Fundamentally, a cost and schedule control system tells management whether a project is over, under, or on budget and schedule at any point in time. A cost and schedule control system is instrumental in identifying problems early, when the solution is least expensive. The cost and schedule control system predicts end dates and total costs based on unforeseen events occurring during the course of the project. The cost and schedule control system is unbiased and provides detailed information about the overall financial and schedule status of the project. Finally, the cost and schedule control system is tied directly to the original financial project plan.

We will go into much more detail in later chapters on how to set up and use a cost and schedule control system, but for now suffice it to say that any good cost and schedule control system must have three components, namely:

❑ The initial financial project plan

❑ A way of determining how much work has been completed against the plan

❑ A way of determining how much it cost to complete the work to date

The cost and schedule control system described in this book has all three components and will be explained completely in Chapter 8, "Managing Cost and Schedule."

(Note that we used the term "financial project plan" in the above discussion to differentiate the information contained in this document from some of the information contained in a traditional project plan. Traditionally, project plans contain more than just financial information. A project plan should be written for all projects, but this book is concerned with creating the financial project plan. Generally, the elements of the financial project plan, as defined in this chapter and, in much greater detail in later chapters, are part of a well-written project plan.)

Support Functions

We have already discussed the importance of estimates, financial project plans, and the cost and schedule control system. These are all extremely important components of delivering a project on time and on budget, but as is the case with all plans and estimates, there are always deviations from the plan once the project starts. They are unavoidable and must be managed. For example, functionality changes or is added as the project evolves. This is inevitable as users change their minds and remember other things that the system must do. Since these changes are inevitable, ultimate success, based on delivering the project on time and on budget, depends on being able to manage and control those changes. This is where the first support function, Configuration Management, comes into play.

A good Configuration Management system not only identifies change, but also quantifies it in terms of cost and schedule impacts. Chapter 9, "Managing Change," covers this subject in detail. In it, you will learn that controlling changes ensures that the initial estimate and financial project plan are updated to reflect the cost and schedule impact associated with changes. The Configuration Management system you will learn about is very flexible and is meant to introduce visibility into changes. Using this system will ensure that when the project is completed, the final cost and end date are as expected, given the changes made to the original plans.

The Configuration Management system also ensures that key stakeholders, such as the executive owning the project's budget and the business leader whose organization will ultimately use the system, agree to these changes before they are implemented. If changes do impact the final cost and end date, the Configuration Management system ensures that no one is surprised by the final cost and completion date.

Another support function is Quality Assurance. Newly developed software with inherent quality issues requires more testing and rework to make the final product acceptable. Extra testing and rework wreaks havoc on the initial cost and schedule estimates, causing both to be significantly different from what was originally promised. In recognition of this, all projects should implement a Quality Assurance process. Building quality into a new software product is an easy and effective technique that contributes immensely toward completing the project on time and on budget.

Since quality can be a significant factor in overall cost and schedule success, it is covered extensively in Chapter 10, "Managing Quality." When reading about Quality Assurance, you will learn how to build quality into the software so that quality problems do not plague your final product.

As you will see after reading the "Managing Quality" chapter, the approach to quality goes way beyond just testing. Of course, testing is a very important aspect of a good Quality Assurance program, but it is not the only aspect. In reality, quality must be built into the project long before it reaches the testing phase. Building quality into the project during the entire life cycle helps prevent costly reworks of poor quality later. This approach helps the project manager adhere to the original project plan.

Book Overview

Let us briefly outline the entire process of planning and managing a software development effort. In later chapters we will look at the topics discussed below in detail.

Completing a project on time and on budget consists of the following steps:

❏ Executive planning

❏ Detailed planning

❏ Project management

Executive Planning

The Executive Planning phase begins the planning effort. The intent of the Executive Planning phase is to document the overall scope of the project. For example, is the new system an extension of an existing website or a completely new one? Does the new system interface with the legacy accounting system? What are the overall functions of the new system? When does the project have to be completed?

In addition to identifying the project's basic functionality, a second focus of the Executive Planning phase is to create a Statement of Work. A Statement of Work documents all the tasks that must be done in order to complete the project. These include not only development tasks, but also non-development tasks such as preparing user training material.

Using the Statement of Work and a definition of the project's scope, estimators can make a rough estimate of the project's total cost. Having the cost estimate also makes it possible to estimate an end date for the project. The cost estimate and the end date are two pieces of information needed to conduct feasibility analysis on the new system. Feasibility analysis is the third task completed during the Executive Planning phase and is used to determine whether the project is worth the time, effort, and cost.

There are three different types of feasibility analysis with which we shall concern ourselves. These are: financial, technical, and schedule feasibility. Based on the rough estimate for the project, executives can determine whether the project is financially and technically feasible and whether the overall schedule is feasible in terms of supporting the business's needs.

Detailed Planning

If the project is feasible on all accounts, the executive responsible for the project approves the next step of the project, which is the Detailed Planning phase.

During the Detailed Planning phase, a set of system requirements is collected. These requirements are based on the initial functionality identified during the Executive Planning phase but go into much greater detail. The system requirements serve two important functions. First, they provide a clear and unambiguous definition of what the new system must do, and second, they are used as the basis for a very detailed cost and schedule estimate.

The detailed cost and schedule estimates derived during the Detailed Planning phase are based on the system requirements and provide refinements to the rough or high-level cost and schedule estimates created during the Executive Planning phase. Since the system requirements provide a great deal of insight into the functionality and operational characteristics of the new system, the estimate based on them is inherently more accurate than the one created earlier. Complete details on creating a detailed cost estimate are contained in Chapter 4, "Estimating Costs."

This final estimate, although very accurate, cannot be used to manage a project because it is simply a bucket of dollars or hours. It does not specify when those dollars or hours get spent or how many resources are needed. As mentioned earlier, the estimate is not a financial project plan. Because of this fact, the next task in the Detailed Planning phase is to create a financial project plan based on the newly created and more accurate cost and schedule estimates.

The first step in this process is to convert the cost estimate to a time-phased resource load. This indicates how many people are needed on the project and when they are needed. Generally, the time-phased resource load uses a month as the increment of time. For each month, the time-phased resource load shows the number and type of personnel working on the project. For example, the time-phased resource load for a small, six-month-long project might show that during the first month there are two architects assigned to the project. In month two, three coders are added. During the third month the number of coders goes up by one–and so on. The time-phased resource load is explained in much more detail in Chapter 5, "Determining the Budget."

Once the time-phased resource load is complete, it is converted to a time-phased budget that shows how much budget is used during each month of the project. This entails assigning an hourly rate to the resources shown in the time phase resource load. Using the above example, if the architects' hourly rates were $50 per hour, then the first month of the time-phased budget would be $16,000. This is based on the assumption that the first month has 160 hours of work time scheduled (40 hours per week times 4 weeks). The $16,000 for the first month is based on the simple equation (2 architects times 160 hours times $50 per hour). In

Chapter 5 you will learn how to create a time-phased budget and time-phased resource load.

Based on the time-phased resource load and the time-phased budget, a detailed project schedule is prepared next. The schedule shows the tasks that must be completed, when those tasks start and stop, and the relationships between the tasks. We will cover the details of how to create a world-class schedule in Chapter 7.

After the time-phased resource load, time-phased budget, and schedule are finished, senior management has another chance to decide whether to proceed with the project. At this point in the planning process, managers have a much more accurate estimate of the total cost of the project in addition to a detailed financial project plan spelling out the number of resources needed, when they are required, and also what the monthly expenditure rate for the project will be.

If senior management decides to proceed with the project, the last step in the Detailed Planning phase is to load the time-phased budget and schedule into a cost and schedule control system. After the project starts, the cost and schedule control system tells management whether the project is on, over, or under budget and also the schedule at any point in time. It is the key management tool used throughout the duration of the project.

Managing the Effort

By following the methodology outlined above, you have accomplished several major feats. First, you have successfully tied the estimate directly to what has to be built (as specified by the system requirements). Second, you have tied the resources needed to complete the project directly to the estimate. Third, you have tied the budget (the time-phased budget) for the project directly to the number of resources needed. Finally, you have tied your cost and schedule control system directly to your budget. You will manage your project according to a very accurate financial plan based on exactly what users want you to build. Every aspect of the estimate, budget, and management system is directly related and integrated. These relationships are the pillars upon which you will successfully complete your project on time and on budget.

Now that you have an idea of how everything ties together and also an idea of the importance of the initial project estimate, it is time to look into the details and to learn how to do those things. We will start with Executive Planning, the subject of the next chapter.

CHAPTER 2

Executive Planning

Software systems begin as an idea to either meet a business need or to improve on the way a need is currently met. Once this need has been identified and a software system is approved to meet the need, organizations begin to conduct a host of activities such as designing, coding, and testing to bring the new system on line. Future users of the new system and executives expect the project to be completed successfully. Everyone wants the project finished on time and on budget as promised.

The first step in delivering any project on time and on budget involves planning all aspects of the project. This includes determining the scope of the project, the budget, and the schedule. In this book we will use a two-phased planning approach. The first phase is called Executive Planning, and the second phase is called Detailed Planning.

The purpose of the Executive Planning phase is to determine the scope of the project and to create a rough or high level estimate of the total cost to complete the project. Based on the estimated cost and scope, management can determine whether the project is feasible. If the project is feasible, then the project enters the second phase of planning, namely, Detailed Planning.

During the Detailed Planning phase the initial project's scope, cost, and schedule estimates are refined significantly. The result is a very detailed description of the project's scope documented in a set of system requirements and very accurate cost and schedule estimates that are converted to a financial project plan.

Executive Planning is the topic of this chapter. Detailed Planning is covered in following chapters.

Typically, Executive Planning is characterized by a set of steps undertaken by the organization to determine the project's scope and budget estimate. These steps vary from company to company. For our purposes the Executive Planning phase consists of the following seven steps:

1. Identifying the business need

2. Writing a Technical Requirements Specification

3. Creating a Statement of Work

4. Baselining the Technical Requirement Specification and Statement of Work

5. Creating a rough estimate of the project's cost and schedule

6. Performing feasibility analysis

7. Making a go/no-go decision on moving to the next step

We will discuss each of these steps below.

Step 1 — Identifying the Business Need

The first phase in the executive planning sequence is to qualify and quantify a business need requiring new software to implement.

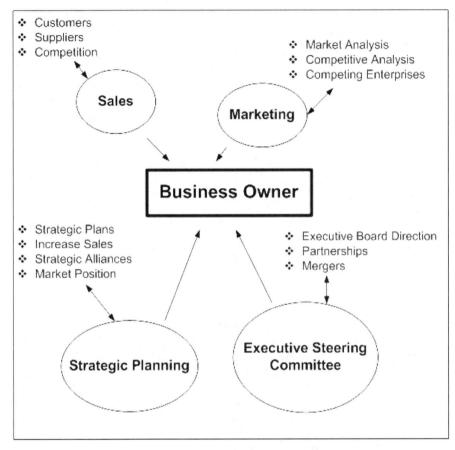

Figure 2-1 Business Need Identification

As shown in Figure 2-1, business needs can come from a variety of sources depending on how the enterprise is organized.

For example, in a sales driven organization, the sales group's vice president may be getting input indicating that customers would rather buy products via the Internet rather than use the company's catalog. This might be driven by 24-hour-a-day operations where products need to be purchased any time of the day, any day of the week.

Other groups generating requirements for a new project include:

Marketing

The Marketing group provides requirements for things such as customer profiling, catalog creation and maintenance, email campaigning, coupons, advertisement keying, pricing, and discounting. Marketing requirements are often also embedded in data warehousing requirements.

Strategic Planning

The Strategic Planning organization provides requirements dealing with business strategy, such as how a new system provides a competitive advantage. An example of a strategic planning requirement might be how the system will help meet long-term strategic goals, such as generating 20 percent of total revenues from Internet sales.

Executive Steering Committee

The Executive Steering Committee often works closely with the strategic planning organization to determine top-level project requirements, such as how the project should be used to reduce total operating cost or specifying a Return On Investment (ROI) for the new project.

As shown in Figure 2-1 above, any group can create a business requirement for a new system.

As a matter of nomenclature, the group that champions the project, that is, the group that comes forward and says, "We need this project," is called the *Business Owner*. Generally, the Business Owner is an individual who represents the group requesting the project.

In some cases, the role of Business Owner might be shared by two or more groups, but in these cases, one group should be designated as the primary group and assume the role of the Business Owner, coordinating the requirements of the other group or groups.

Step 2 — Writing a Technical Requirements Specification

Once a business need has been identified and all the stakeholders agree that a new software system must be built to meet the need, the next step in the Executive Planning process is to determine the scope of the project. This is accomplished by writing a Technical Requirements Specification (TRS). The TRS describes things such as the high level functions of the system, users of the system, the business case for the system, and other pieces of information. Keep in mind that the information in the TRS is high level and is used for planning purposes, not for building the system.

A table of contents for a typical TRS would include:

❑ New system overview

❑ Current system definition

❑ New system definition

❑ Impacts of the new system

❑ Advantages and disadvantages of the new system

❑ Notes

Each of these items is discussed in the following sections.

New System Overview

The first topic covered in the TRS is an overview of the new system. Things to include when writing the overview are:

❑   An outline of the new functionality the system provides

❑   A discussion of how the system improves the enterprise's competitive position

❏ A summary of the project's sponsors and stake holders

❏ An identification of end users

❏ An identification of the installation site

These are all important aspects when considering what the new system should really do for the enterprise. Everyone involved with the system must read and agree with the system overview, including end users and the owner of the budget for the project.

Although short, the above list provides adequate points of discussion for defining the new system. If the items mentioned above are seriously considered, the enterprise will be much further along in defining the new system than if these items are ignored.

Current System Definition

If an existing system(s) is being replaced or supplemented, the functions of that system must be fully understood. This analysis serves two purposes. First, it helps guarantee that the overall capabilities of the legacy system are not regressed or omitted. Second, if done correctly, this type of analysis goes a long way toward showing the strengths and weaknesses of the current system.

The new system should be built around the strengths of the old system, and weaknesses of the old system should be addressed and corrected. Many times, older systems have features that users really like. Removing these from the new system is a serious mistake. Strengths should be duplicated, and weaknesses should be eliminated.

When performing this type of analysis consider the following:

Operational Environment of Existing Hardware — This includes items such as servers and, in some cases, mainframes. Other considerations are the geographical location of the existing system and whether the new system will be hosted in the same environment.

Interfaces With Other Systems — "Other Systems" can include legacy systems that will not be replaced as well as other systems such as database systems. In the case of business-to-business operations, the other business' systems must be considered.

Maintenance Costs of the Existing Hardware and Software — All systems have associated maintenance costs that should be determined before the new system is developed. A major objective of all new development efforts is lowering maintenance costs. Obviously, this goal cannot be attained if the current costs of operation are not known.

Capabilities of the Existing System — As mentioned above, the current system capabilities must be very well understood before the new system is developed. This helps ensure that no capability is missed and also helps when developing the budget by making it possible to separate new requirements from existing requirements.

Performance Characteristics of the Existing System — Like capabilities mentioned above, the performance of the existing system must be very well understood in terms of both strengths and weaknesses. For example, an old system based on a client/server architecture is probably very fast. Similar performance will be expected from the new system as well.

Reliability, Maintainability, Availability, Flexibility, Portability, and Usability of the Existing System — How well the old system held up and how easy it was to maintain are also key considerations. When looking at these features of a legacy system, you may come across parts of the old system that cause problems. Replacing these weak links is often quite easy in the new system.

Provisions for Safety, Security, and Emergency Operations — In many industries where software is used, safety is probably not a consideration. However, security will almost always be a very important aspect of a system. Understanding how security or safety is handled in the old system provides a baseline measurement for improvement in the new system.

Operational Considerations — The Technical Requirements Specification can also be used to collect operational information such as:

❏ Personnel involved in using and operating the current system

❏ Support concept for the current system

The new system should not require more resources and effort to maintain and operate than the existing system. As a matter of fact, a design goal for any new project is the reduction of all costs associated with doing business.

New System Definition

Once the preliminaries are out of the way, the real work of writing the Technical Requirements Specification begins. Start with the key characteristics of the new system. These can usually be grouped into the major areas defined below:

Scope of New System

Include background information on the new system, and establish a clear understanding of what the new system should and should not do.

Operations Policies

Describe changes in the way your enterprise will conduct business when using the new system. For instance, customers may be able to get information that was not previously available. This might have a significant impact on the organization.

Functions of the New System

Include all the major functions of the new system, such as inventory control, order fulfillment, order entry, accounting, etc.

Operational Environment

Specify the hardware environment envisioned for the new system, including the type of operating and database systems required.

Major External Interfaces
Include interfaces with existing systems and interfaces with new systems, such as those used at a supplier.

Inputs and Outputs
Define inputs and outputs to establish boundaries for the new system.

Performance Characteristics
Answer the questions, "How much and how fast?" When looking at performance, focus not only on the average performance requirements, but also on peak requirements. For many projects, peak times can be daily or seasonal, such as between Thanksgiving and Christmas.

Quality Attributes
Include attributes such as maintainability, reliability and scalability. Also include security and safety requirements. Taken in this context, maintainability applies to how easy the system is to fix or upgrade. Reliability deals with the overall robustness of the system while scalability pertains to how easily the system can be modified to handle increased performance requirements.

Users/Customers
Identify new users of the system, any training required for those users, and required changes to the functional organizations when the new system becomes operational. When talking about customers, it is important to take a very broad view of what a customer is. For example, if the new system has elements of Business-to-Business commerce not contained in the old system, then the other businesses should be considered customers or users of the new system.

Support Concept
Identify support personnel, facilities, hardware, and maintenance schedules. It is particularly important to understand completely the support concept of systems that require a 24/7 operational environment. Around-the-clock operation puts special requirements on the availability of the system, especially when upgrades are expected.

Based on the above discussion, you might be drawn to the conclusion that a well-written Technical Requirements Specification negates the need for a rigorous system analysis phase. This is not true. The requirements and ideas contained in the system concept are high level and broad in scope. The idea is not to write a system analysis document, but rather to gain an understanding of how the new system will operate and also to include the major functions required from it.

Impacts of the New System

Any new system introduced into a business will have impacts on the company. These include not only how users interact with the new system, but also the new workflows required to support the system. A good Technical Requirements Specification considers these impacts with a focus on streamlining and improving business operations. Items to cover include:

Operational Impacts — Include impacts on users and support personnel. Operational impacts also include impacts on existing interfaces, computer centers, procedures, and data use. Data impacts include changes such as quantity, timeliness and retention periods of data.

Be sure to identify any legacy data currently contained in the old system and required by the new system. This analysis provides a good idea of the cost associated with data conversion efforts.

Organizational Impacts — Describe the anticipated impacts to existing organizations. A key aspect of many new systems is to allow organizations to downsize and streamline operations. If this is a primary consideration, these types of organizational impacts must be fully described. Also, it is important to identify how workflows will be modified to accommodate the new system.

Other Impacts — Describe the impacts on users, developers, and the enterprise's overall business resulting from the development effort. For example, consider the impacts and changes to databases, training, and any impacts resulting from parallel operations of the new and legacy systems. One area to be particularly concerned with are the impacts resulting from new system test and verification activities.

Advantages and Disadvantages of the New System

This is the section to describe the advantages and disadvantages of the new system. When preparing this part of the Technical Requirements Specification, you might include:

Advantages
Provide a qualitative and quantitative summary of the advantages the new system provides. Include new capabilities, enhanced capabilities, and improved performance.

Disadvantages
New systems are not panaceas for everything that ails a business. Temper expectations with realistic assessments of the limitations of the new system, such as increased hardware, organization impacts, degraded performance, and/or removed capabilities.

Alternatives
Include alternative hardware selections, such as workstations or mainframes, and alternative system architectures, such as client/server applications. Specify the advantages and disadvantages of each as well as a rationale for considering the alternative. In some cases, there might be commercially available software systems that can be purchased. This is the section to explore these possibilities.

Notes

This is a good place to cover information that has not been included elsewhere. Assumptions, rough cost estimates, schedules, and supporting design information are all things that might show up in this section.

Other things to include are charts, performance characteristics, and notes detailing decisions of importance.

Step 3 — Creating a Statement of Work

As work on the Technical Requirement Specification continues, the Statement of Work (SOW) can be written.

Remember, a key product of the Executive Planning phase is a rough estimate of the total cost to complete the project. To make this estimate, estimators need to know every task that has to be completed during the life of the project. Every task must be estimated. This is where the Statement of Work is used. The Statement of Work lists all the tasks that must be completed in order to build the new software system. These tasks include development tasks, such as analysis, design, coding, and testing, as well as non-development tasks, such as Project Management, Quality Assurance, and Configuration Management.

The purpose of identifying these tasks is so that they can be estimated. Obviously, estimating the total project cost involves understanding all the tasks that must be completed.

Shown below are many of the tasks typically included in a well-written Statement of Work:

❏ Analysis

❏ Design

❏ Coding

❏ Testing

❏ Prototyping

❏ Project management

❏ Risk management

❑   Travel

❑   Trade studies

❑   Quality Assurance

❑   Training

❑   Contractor management

❑   Networking

❑   Reviews

❑   Meetings

❑   Reports (status reports, financial reports, etc.)

❑   Procurement activities

❑   Data conversion

Notice that many of these tasks are easily forgotten if not captured in the Statement of Work.

When planning a new development effort, use the list above as a checklist of tasks that will have to be estimated and completed prior to delivering the system. Taking this approach will save you from budgetary surprises later in the project resulting from tasks that were forgotten when the initial estimate was made.

Relationship Between the Statement of Work and the Project Life Cycle

A Statement of Work includes all the tasks required to complete the project. Included are development tasks such as designing, coding and testing the system. These tasks are listed in the Statement of Work because an estimate in dollars and hours to complete these tasks must be determined.

With that in mind, it is important to decide what type of development life cycle will be used for the project. This information is needed because each step in the project's life cycle, regardless of the type of life cycle chosen, becomes a task that must be estimated and consequently listed in the Statement of Work. For example, if for whatever reason, a waterfall life cycle is chosen for a new development effort, then tasks that would be listed on the Statement of Work would include Analysis, Design, Coding, and Testing. If an iterative life cycle is chosen, then some means must be used to estimate the duration of the iterations. If your life cycle calls for a prototyping effort, then the prototyping must be included in the Statement of Work.

There are many types of life cycles, so it is important to choose one that is most likely to lead to successful completion of the project and include all the life cycle steps in the Statement of Work.

Statement of Work Structure

The easiest way to understand the structure of a Statement of Work is to look at an example.

Consider, for a moment, a company that sells widgets. The company's executives decide they need an Internet presence to sell their products. This means starting a new project that, when completed, will allow the company's customers to view an online catalog, search for a widget, and order it — a fairly straightforward development effort. After a great deal of debate, management finally decides to call the project the Catalog Ordering System. On this hypothetical project, the Statement of Work might look like that shown in Figure 2-2.

For a small project like the one described in this example, this Statement of Work adequately covers everything needed to design, build, test, and deploy the new system.

Notice how the Statement of Work is hierarchical in nature and that it resembles an outline with progressive detail shown at the lower levels. Also notice that the top item is the system itself. Approaching the Statement of Work in this manner makes it much

SOW ELEMENTS

1.0.0	CATALOG ORDERING SYSTEM
1.1.0	Project Management
1.1.1	General Management
1.1.2	Review Support
1.2.0	Risk Management
1.2.1	Risk Management Plan
1.2.2	Ongoing Risk Management
1.3.0	Documentation
1.3.1	Requirements Specifications
1.3.2	Design Documentation
1.4.0	Site Development
1.4.1	System Analysis
1.4.2	System Design
1.4.3	CI Analysis
1.4.4	CI Design
1.4.5	Coding
1.4.6	Data Conversion
1.5.0	Facilities
1.5.1	Production Server Facility
1.5.2	Development Facility
1.6.0	Test and Evaluation
1.6.1	Development Testing
1.6.2	Factory Testing
1.6.3	Site Testing
1.7.0	Configuration Management
1.7.1	Identification
1.7.2	Control
1.7.3	Audits
1.7.4	Status Accounting
1.8.0	Quality Assurance
1.8.1	Procedure Compliance
1.8.2	Plan Compliance
1.8.3	Test Review

Figure 2-2 Statement of Work for the Catalog Ordering System

easier to ensure that all the necessary tasks are covered. And, as we will see later, using the hierarchical approach makes collecting and summarizing cost estimates easier.

Creating a Statement of Work Dictionary

The Statement of Work dictionary, as the name implies, provides definitions for all the tasks shown in the Statement of Work. This ensures that everyone understands what a task entails. For example, the Statement of Work dictionary entry for Project Management might look something like the following:

1.1.0 Project Management

1.1.1 General Management — Consists of all the tasks required to plan and coordinate the development effort. This also includes the effort required to ensure the technical excellence of the project and to ensure that the project is completed on time and on budget.

1.1.2 Review Support — This task includes all the effort required to prepare for and to conduct the following formal reviews:

❑ Requirements Review

❑ Design Review

❑ Test Readiness Review

For all items shown in the Statement of Work, the Statement of Work dictionary provides enough information so that each task can be correctly costed. In some cases, ambiguity in defining a task can lead to bad cost estimates. The Statement of Work dictionary is intended to prevent this type of mistake from occurring.

Step 4 — Baselining the TRS and Statement of Work

Once the Statement of Work and TRS are complete, all stakeholders formally approve them. This is typically done at an Executive Planning Meeting attended by the director or manager of every functional organization involved in the project. In many cases, these are the same people whose groups contributed to the Statement of Work and TRS during their creation and, for these people, the meeting should be nothing more than a rubber stamp of products with which they are already familiar.

So why have the Executive Planning Meeting in the first place if it is nothing more than a rubber-stamping exercise? The answer is to let senior management know both that the team has reached an agreement on how the project is going to proceed and that all of the key players have bought into the final plan.

After the Executive Planning Meeting has been completed, key individuals such as the president of the enterprise will know that everyone involved has agreed to the end dates and committed their organizations to doing the project within the allocated budget.

In most cases there will be few reasons to update the Statement of Work or TRS. This is because of the fact that once the project starts, the Statement of Work and TRS are replaced with other more detailed documents. We will learn about that phase in later chapters.

However, a key circumstance that requires updating of the Statement of Work and TRS is when the scope of the project changes. Obviously, if the project's scope changes, and the change is significant, all aspects of the Statement of Work and TRS must be evaluated for cost impacts.

Step 5 — Creating a Rough Estimate of the Project's Cost and Schedule

Once the Statement of Work and the Technical Requirement Specification are finished, the next step is to use them to make a rough estimate of the project's total cost.

The reason this estimate is rough or high level, is that there is not yet enough information to estimate the project's cost accurately, but there is enough information to make a rough estimate. The purpose of the rough estimate is to give executives an idea of the project's cost. This information is used in feasibility analysis (covered later in this chapter) to decide whether to proceed. If the enterprise decides to proceed with the project, then a more accurate estimate for the project is created in the Detailed Planning phase following the Executive Planning phase.

Creating a project estimate entails estimating the cost for each task on the Statement of Work. For example, by using the Technical Requirements Specification, the amount of effort needed to design the new system (in this example, *design* is a task on the Statement of Work) can be roughly estimated. Similarly, once the total estimate for the project has been determined, the amount of Project Management time can be estimated. In this manner, by looking at the tasks in the Statement of Work and also by understanding the Technical Requirements for the project, a total estimate for the project is created.

Development tasks can be estimated in a variety of ways. However, in all cases some aspect of the estimate is based on professional judgment. Key individuals, who have built similar types of systems, must provide input on how long it will take to complete a task such as coding. This estimate is based on their experience and judgment.

Since the estimate is based on professional judgment, it is subject to error. One effective way of minimizing estimating error is to have other senior personnel review it. Having others look at the estimate usually enhances its accuracy.

Another way to enhance the accuracy of an estimate is to be sure that the estimators have experience with that sort of project. Someone with extensive experience building order entry systems might have a hard time estimating the cost of building an accounting system.

Other non-development tasks on the Statement of Work also have to be estimated. For example, travel estimates are made by estimating how many trips are required, how many people will travel, and the approximate cost per trip.

Configuration Management and Quality Assurance tasks are usually estimated as a percentage of the total project.

We will not get into details on how to estimate Statement of Work tasks in this chapter since guidelines on estimating are provided in Chapter 4, "Estimating Costs." Although the cost estimating techniques explained in that chapter are for the Detailed Planning phase, they are equally applicable during the Executive Planning phase. The only difference is the degree of accuracy needed for each phase.

Constraints

When making the rough project estimate, you should take into account things such as cost constraints, schedule constraints, resource constraints, and organizational dependencies. Each of these items has the potential to influence the project's estimate. We will briefly cover each below.

Cost Constraints

There are usually some cost constraints on a project. Executives might decide that the project must be done for under $500,000 because of budget limitations. This figure might include funding constraints by quarter and/or by fiscal year. See Figure 2-3.

At this point you might be wondering how any budget constraints can be known when the purpose of the Statement of Work is to define the tasks that must be costed in the first place.

The answer is that in the real world, senior management usually has an idea of what the project should cost, or at the very least an idea of the cost that cannot be exceeded. In many cases, as the Statement of Work evolves and actual estimates are determined, this executive management number will have to be adjusted up or down — usually up.

Cost Constraints can be specified in a number of ways such as:

❏ Total project budget

❏ Budget by quarter

❏ Budget by fiscal year

Figure 2-3 Cost Contraints

The purpose of considering cost constraints is to provide an idea of how much budget has been allocated to the project. This helps the estimator determine whether management wants a high-end system or expects a bare-bones system.

In many cases, as the tasks are defined and the basis of estimates are determined, the expected budget numbers have to be refined. This involves an iterative process between management and those providing cost estimates in order to arrive at a common ground where the anticipated budget equals the costs of the tasks to be performed. In some cases, tasks might have to be deleted or deferred to later quarters or years in order to make the budget numbers match.

Schedule Constraints

Like budget constraints, all projects have Schedule Constraints, as shown in Figure 2-4. These are critical dates, usually set by the business owner, based on strategic, political, or market-driven considerations. However, business owners do not have to build and test the system, so it is important that those involved in building the system agree to these need-by dates.

In some instances, these dates must be changed. Schedule is usually king on projects, but, in many cases, business owners cannot predict with accuracy when the project will be completed. Those reviewing the Statement of Work can provide better insight (based on the project estimate) into the end dates, and the schedule can be modified accordingly.

Like the budget numbers, all affected parties must agree to the schedule dates before a decision to proceed is made.

The relationship between schedule constraints and the project estimate is that once the total project estimate has been determined a schedule can also be determined. This schedule can then be compared with the schedule the business owners had in mind, and the two can be modified to coincide.

Resource Constraints

When people talk about resource constraints, they usually are referring to personnel. Many development organizations are paper-thin and do not have the resources to ramp up for a major development effort. As the project estimate evolves, this may become painfully obvious. As the estimate nears completion, it may become obvious that the development organizations do not have the critical skills required to complete the project. See Figure 2-5.

Schedule Constraints can be specified in a number of ways such as:

❑ End date

❑ Key milestones by quarter

❑ Key milestones by year

Figure 2-4
Schedule Contraints

Resource Constraints generally revolve around functional areas such as:

❑ Database programmers

❑ Developers for a specific development language

❑ Key personnel who understand the business rules

Figure 2-5
Resource Contraints

Resource constraints must be considered when making the rough estimate, and a plan must be put into place to eliminate the constraints. Plans can include:

❏ Hiring more personnel

❏ Using staff supplementation

❏ Subcontracting out portions of the project to third-party developers

Other Constraints

In addition to cost, schedule, and resource constraints, other constraints include:

❏ Hardware constraints — such as servers and network capacity

❏ Facility constraints

❏ Legal constraints

❏ Political constraints (internal or external)

❏ Security constraints

❏ Organizational constraints

As was the case with resource constraints, when a constraint is identified, there must be a mitigation plan or a work around plan identified if the project is to be completed successfully.

Organizational Dependencies

Project estimators must also consider the relationships between all of the organizations with a stake in the project's outcome. For example, a key dependency might be that the networking group must procure and install new servers before development on the project begins. This dependency could have the potential to impact the schedule seriously, and eventually the cost of the project, if not realized and documented before the project is started.

In larger enterprises, the number of dependencies can be great, and it is important that all of these interdepartmental dependencies be recognized. In many cases, one group must hand over a product to another group before the second group gets started. These types of dependencies, if not recognized and documented, have the potential to have large and negative impacts on the estimate. Recognizing these dependencies when the estimate is prepared will help ensure that the project starts and progresses smoothly.

Figure 2-6 lists typical enterprise-level departments and the services they provide. Use this as a checklist to help identify potential inter-group dependencies.

As shown in Figure 2-6, many groups have an impact on the project, and these groups need to be identified and the product(s) they provide documented. Departmental dependencies often show up on the schedule and, in many cases, are useful for identifying critical paths.

Using the Statement of Work to Summarize the Project's Budget

Since the Statement of Work identifies all of the tasks needed for a new project, it can be used for budgeting purposes. Using the Statement of Work in this way makes it easier to determine the total cost for each task and then to sum up the costs to get a complete project cost.

For example, the Facilities line item (number 1.5.0 from the Statement of Work in Figure 2-2) consists of two parts, the Production Server Facility and the Development Facility. Based on that information, the total budget for Facilities can be determined from the equation below:

GROUP	SERVICES
Database Group	❑ Installation of new databases ❑ Development of database objects
Web Programmers	❑ Development of presentation layer software
Network Group	❑ Installation of new networking equipment ❑ Upgrading existing networks
Development Organization	❑ Performing analysis ❑ Writing source code
Configuration Management	❑ Providing status accounting ❑ Providing product identification ❑ Providing product control ❑ Providing reports
Quality Assurance	❑ Witnessing formal testing ❑ Conducting product evaluations
Contractor Management	❑ Writing procurement specifications ❑ Managing contractors
Logistics	❑ Determining packaging requirements ❑ Specifying labeling
Legal	❑ Identifying legal issues ❑ Writing site legal disclaimers
Finance	❑ Generating budgets ❑ Maintaining budgets
Procurement	❑ Generating procurement specifications ❑ Selecting vendors
Test	❑ Writing test plans ❑ Writing test procedures ❑ Conducting formal acceptance tests
Graphic Arts	❑ Creating web page layouts ❑ Developing animations ❑ Creating web page graphics

Figure 2-6 Key Organization Elements and their Products

Total Budget for Facilities =

Budget for the Production Server Facility +

Budget for the Development Facility

A similar equation can be used for every item in the Statement of Work, with lower-level items summing up to the higher level items.

As you look at Figure 2-2, notice that the first line in the Statement of Work is the system itself. The Statement of Work is designed to make it possible to sum up the budget from all of the lower levels to get the total cost of the project. In other words, the total budget for the project can be calculated as follows:

Total budget for the *Catalog Ordering System* =

Budget for Project Management +

Budget for Risk Management +

Budget for Documentation +

Budget for Site Development +

Budget for Facilities +

Budget for Test and Evaluation +

Budget for Configuration Management +

Budget for Quality Assurance

Figure 2-7 shows this idea for the Catalog Ordering System Statement of Work using some obviously fictitious numbers to make the math easier.

In Figure 2-7, the budget is given in hours, not dollars. This is the case because we have not yet determined who is going to do the

SOW Tasks		Budget (Hours)	Budget (Hours)	Budget (Hours)
1.0.0	**CATALOG ORDERING SYSTEM**			98
1.1.0	**Project Management**		7	
1.1.1	General Management	3		
1.1.2	Review Support	4		
1.2.0	**Risk Management**		9	
1.2.1	Risk Management Plan	4		
1.2.2	Ongoing Risk Management	5		
1.3.0	**Documentation**		11	
1.3.1	Technical Requirements Specification	5		
1.3.2	Statement of Work	6		
1.4.0	**Site Development**		15	
1.4.1	System Requirements Specification	1		
1.4.2	System Design Specification	2		
1.4.3	Software Requirements Specification	3		
1.4.4	Software Design Specification	4		
1.4.5	Coding	5		
1.4.6	Data Conversion			
1.5.0	**Facilities**		5	
1.5.1	Production Server Facility	2		
1.5.2	Development Facility	3		
1.6.0	**Test and Evaluation**		18	
1.6.1	Development Testing	5		
1.6.2	Factory Testing	6		
1.6.3	Site Testing	7		
1.7.0	**Configuration Management**		18	
1.7.1	Identification	3		
1.7.2	Audits	4		
1.7.3	Control	5		
1.7.4	Status Accounting	6		
1.8.0	**Quality Assurance**		15	
1.8.1	Procedure Compliance	4		
1.8.2	Plan Compliance	5		
1.8.3	Test Review	6		

Figure 2-7 A Statement of Work Showing Budget in Hours

work. A task might take two hundred hours to complete per the Statement of Work, but how much it actually costs depends on the salary of the person doing the work. Actual dollar costs are determined after the estimate in hours has been calculated and the cost of the personnel doing the work has been determined. We are going to skip that step in this chapter to keep things simple, but on a real project you have to do it. In later chapters you will learn how to convert an hour estimate into a dollar estimate. Despite the fact that the material is covered in the chapters dealing with Detailed Planning, the principle is the same and can be used during the Executive Planning phase. On your project, you will have to take the step of converting the hours to dollars during the Executive Planning phase.

Note that there are some tasks that might not have an hour estimate associated with them. An example is the cost of a new server. Procurement costs must be recognized when determining a project estimate and can be added back to the Statement of Work after the other task estimates have been converted to dollars.

Step 6 — Performing Feasibility Analysis

When the project estimate is complete, the enterprise can complete its feasibility studies to determine whether the overall cost/benefit ratio is large enough to justify the time and expense associated with developing a new system.

The reason that the estimate and the Technical Requirements Specification are completed prior to conducting feasibility analysis is that the estimate and technical requirements are needed to conduct most types of feasibility analysis. For example, a key parameter in any type of financial feasibility is the estimated cost of the project. Similarly, one has to know what the technical requirements are before conducting technical feasibility studies.

With that introduction, we can now turn our attention to performing feasibility analysis. For our purposes, we will consider the following types of feasibility analysis:

❑ Technical feasibility

❑ Financial feasibility

❑ Schedule feasibility

Each is discussed below.

Technical Feasibility

Technical feasibility answers several major questions, as shown in Figure 2-8. First, technical feasibility refers to the software development abilities of the enterprise in general. Many companies are not adept at building software even though they have coders on staff. Perhaps these personnel are primarily involved in the maintenance of legacy systems. Suffice it to say that if the organization has never developed a large system from scratch, the technical feasibility of pulling it off successfully is not high.

In cases such as this, it still might be prudent to proceed with the project, but perhaps to contract it out or hire management consultants to run the project.

Another aspect of technical feasibility concerns the technology involved. If the requirements indicate an inordinately high throughput requirement, then the technical staff might determine that this is not technically feasible by any means short of buying a supercomputer. Obviously this approach, for all practical purposes, will not be technically feasible.

Other types of technical feasibility deal with technologies that are just becoming available. For example, in the early days of the Internet, the bandwidth and other technologies were not available to provide streaming video from a website. At that time, streaming video was not technically feasible.

❏ Does the enterprise have the resources to complete this project?

❏ Can the enterprise's IT group complete a project of this scale?

❏ Are the requirements attainable/realistic?

❏ Can the current network and computer infrastructure support this project?

❏ Are any of the requirements "pushing the envelope" in any area (e.g. performance)?

❏ Will the development environment support building this software?

Figure 2-8
Technical Feasibility
Checklist

For many projects, true technical feasibility is seldom an issue. Most requirements levied on business software systems are technically feasible, as opposed to scientific software that often pushes the limits of technical feasibility.

When technical feasibility becomes an issue, it is critical to drill down and to isolate the requirements causing problems. In many cases, one or two troublesome requirements can be eliminated, the result being that a previously unfeasible project becomes once again feasible. Often, deleting these troublesome requirements has no material effect whatsoever on the final product's functionality.

Financial Feasibility

Financial feasibility is another type of feasibility to consider before starting any project of significant size. See Figure 2-9.

Sometimes projects are feasible from a technical or schedule standpoint, but the cost is prohibitive. Completing a financial feasibility analysis upfront will indicate this before a great deal of money is spent developing a project that might not be completed due to a lack of funds.

There are many types of financial feasibility studies that can be conducted. These include financial analyses, such as break-even point, return on investment, and the future value of anticipated revenue streams. Financial feasibility studies are beyond the scope of this book, but

❑ Is the budget available?

❑ Will the budget be available in future periods?

❑ Is the Return On Investment (ROI) adequate?

❑ What is the break-even point?

❑ What is the present and future value of the revenue stream generated by the project?

❑ What are the costs of maintaining the project?

Figure 2-9 Financial Feasibiity Checklist

most books on accounting or finance can provide a background on this type of analysis.

The key point to remember is that senior management must have an idea of the overall cost of the project and confirm that the cost is within the allocated budget for the project.

In the event that cost becomes an issue, some sort of corrective action must be implemented before the project is started. In most cases the only true way to handle cost issues is to de-scope the project. This means taking a hard look at the requirements and making a decision on what must be built and what can either wait or be scrapped.

This approach works well because there is a multiplicative factor associated with requirements. For every requirement, a design must be completed, coded, and tested. The costs of these activities add up. By deleting requirements at the beginning of the project, major cost savings can be realized downstream.

In most cases, reducing scope also reduces risk. The more that has to be built, the more that can go wrong. Keeping it simple is one way to minimize development risks.

Schedule Feasibility

The final type of feasibility analysis revolves around the schedule feasibility of a project, as shown in Figure 2-10. This consideration is often intimately related to considerations such as time to market. Many projects are doable, but not in the time frame key decision makers feel is necessary.

For most projects, time to market is a major issue. If the project takes too long to develop, the competitive advantage for doing the project might be lost. Further, technology changes so rapidly that projects with long lead times tend to become obsolete before they go into operation.

There are several approaches to mitigating schedule issues. The first is to look at the requirements and make sure that they are all necessary. Surprisingly, most projects contain a fair amount of so called "necessary requirements," which are not needed at all. It goes without saying that these requirements take time to build and test.

A second technique for handling schedule feasibility issues is to develop the project in a phased delivery approach. By means of this technique, requirements that are the most critical from a time-to-market standpoint can be developed and put into operation first with the less critical functions following later.

❑ Can the project be finished on time?

❑ Is the completion date supportive of the business goals for the project?

❑ What happens if the project is late?

Figure 2-10 Schedule Feasibility Checklist

Finally, hiring outside consultants to do a portion of the project can mitigate schedule issues. If the project analysis is done correctly, these requirements can be allocated to stand-alone blocks of software that can be built by third-party developers.

In addition to subcontracting out a portion of the project, there is also the option of bringing on outside contractors in a staff supplementation role. Many firms provide these types of services.

One caveat is needed here. Often, decisions are made as to when the project is needed while ignoring key input from developers, such as the fact that the schedule is unrealistic. Unrealistic expectations about schedule feasibility are a major reason why projects are not completed on time. If the developers say a project will be finished third quarter, and management needs it second quarter, the only smart thing to do is to de-scope the second quarter requirements and deliver the less essential functionality in the third quarter. Make no mistake about it, simply demanding a finish date will not get the project done by that date.

Step 7 — Making a Go/No-Go Decision

Once the feasibility analysis is complete, the business owner or key stakeholders make a decision on whether to proceed with the project.

This decision is based on many factors. For example, the project must be technically and financially feasible. In addition, the development schedule must support the business's needs. These determinations are based on the results of the completed feasibility analysis.

If the decision is to proceed, the next step in the process is to begin the Detailed Planning phase. During this phase, a set of system requirements are collected and used in place of the Technical Requirements Specification to define the scope of the project.

Next, a much more accurate project estimate is created based on the system requirements and the Statement of Work. This estimate is used to decide if the project still appears feasible. If it does, then the accurate estimate is converted to a financial project plan, and the project is started.

Now that we know how to complete the Executive Planning phase, we can turn our attention to learning how to complete the Detailed Planning phase of the project. Detailed Planning consists of the following steps:

Step 1: Collect the System Requirements (See chapter 3)

Step 2: Estimate the total project cost (See chapter 4)

Step 3: Determine the budget (See chapter 5)

Step 4: Determine the development organization, and allocate the budget (See chapter 6)

Step 5: Create the schedule (See chapter 7)

As mentioned above, an accurate estimate for the project is determined during the Detailed Planning phase, and the estimate is based on the Statement of Work and the system requirements. Since the system requirements are so important to creating an accurate and detailed project cost and schedule estimate, we will focus our attention on them next. After we know how to gather the system requirements, we will learn how to make a very accurate project estimate, which is the subject of Chapter 4, "Estimating Costs."

Next, we will learn how to convert the estimate into a budget in Chapter 5, and in Chapter 6, we will learn how to determine the optimum project development organization and how to allocate budget to each element of that organization. Finally, in Chapter 7, we will learn how to create the project schedule.

After completing these five chapters, we will have finished our discussion of the Detailed Planning phase and can move on to managing the project.

CHAPTER 3

Collecting System Requirements

AFTER THE EXECUTIVE PLANNING phase is complete, the Detailed Planning phase begins. The end products of the Detailed Planning phase are a set of system requirements and much more accurate cost and schedule estimates for the project based on the system requirements. Since system requirements are crucial for defining what software to build and for accurately estimating the overall cost and schedule for a new project, we will devote a chapter to the topic of how to collect them.

Before we get started, a point about methodology needs to be made. In this chapter, system requirements are discussed from a classical sense. The methodology discussed is based on functional decomposition. This methodology was chosen because it is easy to understand and most readers will be familiar with it. However, any methodology that accurately collects the system requirements can be used. The main point of the current chapter is that the system has to be defined before an accurate estimate of the cost to build the system can be determined. Any approach that provides you with these results will work.

Additionally, as mentioned earlier, system requirements are top-level requirements detailing the functions of the new system. Generally, they are at too high of a level to be used as build-to requirements, but instead serve as a basis from which detailed build-to requirements can be derived.

Having a good set of system requirements serves several purposes. Most importantly, it allows all the requirements for the system to be collected and analyzed at once. This is advantageous since seeing the whole picture upfront ensures that no significant functionality is missed and also ensures a better design.

Equally important, having a complete set of system requirements makes estimating the entire project's development cost more accurate. No one can determine the end cost of developing a major project when all the functional requirements for the new system are not fully understood.

Finally, system requirements are the basis for defining the parts of the system. For example, a system might include both an order entry piece and a fulfillment piece. Analyzing the system requirements would make that clear. Once the system has been defined as having the order entry and fulfillment pieces, the project manager can determine the optimum development organization and assign a total budget and schedule to those organizational elements. We will learn the details on how to do this in Chapter 6.

As an aside, we will call the document containing the system requirements the System Requirements Specification (SRS) throughout this book.

With that said, let us take a look at what is required to complete a world-class system analysis. But first, we need to take a moment to talk about how to find the information needed to write a good requirement.

How to Find Information

The hardest part of developing any software, regardless of whether it is an order entry system or a weather prediction system, is gathering the requirements. Once requirements are accurately collected, building the system typically progresses smoothly. If the project is not going well, the root cause can usually be traced to incomplete, changing, or missing requirements.

Gathering requirements is never easy. This is especially true for new systems where very little is known other than a general outline of what the system should do. As you will see, anyone can use the two steps discussed next to get a very good set of requirements.

Step 1 — Review All Existing Documentation

When collecting requirements for a new system, the first place to start is with existing documentation. Good sources of existing documentation include:

Manuals or Code for Existing Systems

Often, manuals for existing systems can provide insight into interfaces that have to be maintained with other legacy systems. This is important, and sometimes difficult, information to collect.

Additionally, manuals often provide information about hardware requirements, maintenance procedures, user training requirements, and other pertinent facts about a legacy system. In some instances, these requirements might be the same for the new system or at least provide leads as to the types of requirements to consider for the new system.

In addition, it is often useful, but sometimes very difficult, to look at the actual code of a legacy system. Reviewing code is a particularly useful approach when the purpose of a new system is to replace a legacy system. The code for a legacy system will provide complete details on existing and, in many cases, very complicated business rules. Sometimes, subject matter experts might not know this information down to the level of detail required to build a new system.

Note that when considering whether to look at existing code as a source of requirements, two considerations should be taken into account. In some instances, business owners want to replace a system because it is not meeting current business requirements.

Looking at the code from a legacy system and then duplicating that functionality with new technology or hardware may or may not solve the inherent problems with the legacy system.

On the other hand, looking at code can be a particularly effective means of collecting detailed business rules that are still pertinent. Sometimes subject matter experts know what they want, but do not know the low-level details required to achieve those results. Looking at an existing system's code alleviates that problem and, in some cases, is a much faster approach to collecting system requirements than trying to get the same information from a subject matter expert.

Existing Business Forms
These can be used as the basis for understanding input or output to the new system. Often a new system replaces a manual operation. Looking at the forms required to complete these manual operations can tell you a great deal about what the new system must accomplish.

Existing Business Reports
Like forms, existing reports often describe what data users need. Looking at reports is often easier than asking users what they use as information sources on a day-to-day basis.

Organizational Charts and Charters
These can be useful for determining the information needs of different groups as well as how information flows through an organization. Looking over this type of information will also give you a very good idea of who does what and who is responsible for what. This is often a good way to get a head start on finding subject matter experts needed to provide detailed requirements later in the process.

Procedures
Procedures are especially useful for systems designed to replace manual operations. Procedures can be invaluable as they often describe, in detail, the steps to completing a task that will be automated by the new system.

Step 2 — Use Subject Matter Experts

Gathering information from subject matter experts can also be difficult for a variety of reasons. Sometimes these individuals are unwilling to take the time needed to provide a complete set of requirements. Other times these people might not realize how important some facts are and not mention them, perhaps thinking that the analysts must already know such an obvious point. And, of course, there is always the worst-case scenario, where subject matter experts do not feel the need to cooperate for one reason or another.

Described below are some techniques you can use to overcome these difficulties.

Interviews
Interviews can either be singular or conducted in groups. Regardless of the approach taken, there are four key activities associated with any interview. They are:

❑ Prepare the interview questions

❑ Conduct the interview

❑ Analyze the data gathered during the interview

❑ Follow up for clarification where required

Each of these activities is self-explanatory, so we need say no more about them here. However, there are pros and cons associated with an interview that you should understand prior to deciding on this approach. Pros of Using an Interview:

❑ Collects in-depth material

❑ Allows for follow-up questions for clarification

❑ Gathers very specific information

Cons of Using an Interview:

❑ Time consuming

❑ Some situations permit only interviewing one subject matter expert at a time

❑ Must be very careful about selecting the questions

Questionnaires

Another approach to gathering information from subject matter experts is to prepare a questionnaire. Questionnaires must be carefully thought out; otherwise, they will not be effective.

When designing the questions on a questionnaire, you can take one of two basic approaches. They are:

Use Open-Ended Questions

These take the form of, "Tell me about your job," or "What types of accounting data do you need to do your job?" Open-ended questions can be dangerous, as a subject matter expert might not give the expected answers. However, they can be quite effective when they allow the subject matter expert to elaborate on his or her area of expertise without being fenced in by more restrictive closed-ended questions.

Use Close-Ended Questions

Close-ended questions are designed to gather specific information, such as "How many widgets were sold between Thanksgiving and Christmas last year?" The advantage is that they do not confuse the subject matter expert. The disadvantage is that they do not allow a great deal of leeway for explanations.

Observations

A third way to gather information is to watch subject matter experts do their jobs. This entails sitting down with them for several days or weeks and watching what they do. This would include identifying the reports they use or generate and from whom they get information.

Observations, like interviews and questionnaires, have advantages and disadvantages. The advantage is that if done correctly, observations usually provide a very complete picture of what the subject matter expert needs to get the job done.

The disadvantages are that observations can be time consuming and usually require that the observer have some idea of what is important and what is not. Another disadvantage of observations is that they are usually narrow in scope. After all, it would be difficult to observe everything in even a simple enterprise.

How To Write a System Requirement

You might think that writing a requirement would not be a very difficult task, but nothing could be further from the truth. Writing good requirements is an art that takes practice and knowledge of some basic rules.

Rule #1 — All Requirements Shall Contain the Word "Shall"

Why the word "shall" you might ask? The reason is simple. All requirements that have the word "shall" in them have to be implemented. If you use some other word, such as "will," it implies that the requirement is a design goal that might not be met. "Shalls" have to be implemented.

Another thing about requirements specified with the word "shall" is that you can develop a test case for each. When you are done testing the system, if all the "shalls" have been successfully tested, the system will be completely tested from a functional standpoint. An important point to remember is that the "shall" level testing is in addition to all the development-level testing, which has to be done to catch bugs. However, from a system standpoint, if all the "shalls" are successfully tested, the developers have built everything needed. No one can come back and say, "You did not do this or that."

Rule #2 — Avoid Ambiguity

Ambiguity is one of the hardest things to remove from requirements because, to the person writing the requirement, it may seem perfectly clear and totally unambiguous. The problem is that the person writing the requirement is often not the person who has to read it later and then write software to implement it. Everyone involved in the requirements process has to learn to recognize requirement ambiguity.

One example of ambiguity revolves around adjectives such as "good," "fast," and "easy." The problems with these types of requirements are that they cannot be tested, and two different people will probably have two different definitions of what they mean. Consider the following requirement:

The system shall be easy to use.

This is obviously a very ambiguous requirement. How is "easy to use" tested? Further, "easy to use" for you might not mean "easy to use" for me. Instead of using the words "easy to use," one should specify exactly what that means. One way of rewording the above requirement would be:

The graphical user interface for the system shall have the look and feel of a standard Windows program.

This implies that there are objects such as a File button and an Edit button in the menu bar at the top of the main window. This is something that could be tested and, further, there are style guides for the look and feel of a Windows program.

Other forms of ambiguity are more difficult to catch. Consider the following, although an admittedly contrived requirement:

The system shall count off ten units.

If the new system interfaces with another system, this type of requirement might cause a problem because the developer does not know whether the counting starts at zero and ends at nine or starts at one and ends at ten.

In all cases, look at the requirement and ask yourself if it can be interpreted in more than one way. If it can, you have ambiguity that needs to be removed.

Rule #3 — Eliminate Compound Requirements

Remember compound sentences from your grade school days? If you do not, compound sentences are sentences in which two independent clauses are joined by a coordinating conjunction, such as "and," "but," "yet," or "so."

In the world of requirements, always rewrite compound requirements in the form:

The system shall do X and shall do Y.

This type of requirement needs to be broken down into two parts to make allocating the requirement to code simpler and to make testing easier.

Do not confuse compound requirements with complicated or broad-based requirements. A requirement that seems to cover a lot of ground may be acceptable because it can be broken down into more parts later in the analysis process.

Rule #4 — Stay Consistent

Amazingly enough, inconsistency is often one of the biggest problems with requirements and also one of the easiest to avoid.

Some areas to focus on are:

❏ **Units of measure** — If you have a requirement specified in metric units, do not specify another in English units.

❏ **Naming conventions** — If you call the end user a "user" in one requirement, do not refer to him or her as a "customer" somewhere else.

❏ **Acronyms** — Do not use the same acronym to mean two different things in different requirements. Be sure to spell out the acronym the first time it is used, and be sure to include a list of acronyms at the back of your document.

❏ **Legacy systems** — Give a legacy system one name and stick to it.

❏ **Divisions within the enterprise** — Call the "East Coast Data Center" the same thing throughout your systems requirements document.

Rule #5 — Do Not Use Names
Do not say, "John shall use the system. . ." Instead, say, "Accounting shall use the system." This is because in the future there will most likely still be an Accounting department, but John might not be part of it.

Rule #6 — Make It Understandable
This is similar to ambiguity, but has a slightly different flavor. Be sure that the developer, who has to implement the requirement with a design and code, can understand exactly what the subject matter expert wanted when the requirement was written.

Rule #7 — Be Sure It Is Testable
Every requirement has to be tested. Be sure the requirement is written in such a manner that it can indeed be tested.

Rule #8 — Be Sure It Is Necessary
Be sure every requirement is necessary. Do not throw in a lot of "bells and whistles." More requirements mean more code, more testing, more cost, and longer development schedules. Only include the requirements that are truly necessary.

If you follow these rules throughout the analysis process, then the following design and coding phases will be a lot easier.

Now that we know how to write a requirement, let us turn our attention to spelling out exactly what types of requirements are needed to define and estimate the cost for the new system

Types of Requirements

When gathering system-level requirements for a new system, the analyst must take into consideration a wide range of requirements that are beyond what typically comes to mind for most people. For example, security requirements might be a significant factor driving design and should be considered when writing the System Requirements Specification. We will start at the top and cover everything you need in the following sections.

System Capabilities

The first place to start when defining requirements at any level is with the basic capabilities of the new system. However, there are actually three types of capability requirements to consider. They are:

❑ Functional requirements

❑ Performance requirements

❑ Data requirements

Although related, the three types of requirements are actually different in nature. We will cover each below, starting with functional requirements.

Functional Requirements
Functional requirements are the functions the system must perform and are what many people think about when they think about defining requirements. Functional requirements cover all aspects of the new system.

When defining functional requirements, state each requirement in an unambiguous way, and make sure it is testable. All the rules for defining requirements covered earlier are applicable. Remember to avoid verbiage, such as "the system shall maximize. . .," which is not testable, but will certainly lead to subsequent disputes about what was really intended.

Functional requirements are the backbone of a new system. Because of that there is a tendency to go into too much detail when these requirements are defined. Remember, system-level requirements are broken down to lower-level requirements after the project starts. During the Detailed Planning phase, focus on the high-level system requirements, and make sure that every requirement that goes into the System Requirements Specification is truly a system-level requirement.

Performance Requirements
Closely related to functional requirements are performance requirements. These are the requirements defining the speed of the new system, such as the number of transactions per minute with a certain number of users on the system.

Functional requirements often have an associated performance requirement, and it is sometimes difficult to tell one from the other. The point here is not necessarily to separate performance and functional requirements, but rather to make sure that when the System Requirements Specification is being written, performance is considered.

In this regard, be sure to think through your performance requirements carefully. For example, make sure that you consider the performance requirements during peak times of the day or during peak seasonal periods. If your system is based on consumer products and purchases, the performance requirements might be much higher between Thanksgiving and Christmas than at other times of the year. Furthermore, peak day-to-day performance requirements have to be thought through carefully in order to take into account the time difference between the East and West coasts and whether the primary end users are people who work or people who are home throughout the day.

Of equal importance, be sure all of the performance requirements can be met. When in doubt, use a "To Be Determined (TBD)." Follow this up with a trade study or a prototype to determine the correct value. Often, performance requirements will drive design, especially in the area of scalability, and should be given thought up front. Nothing is worse than coming up with a requirement that cannot be met.

Also, be sure that all the performance requirements can be tested. This might require that test software be written to stress the system with the anticipated number of peak transactions. The testability issue might also require that some sort of mathematical analysis be used in the testing phase if the only true way to test the requirement is with the production system.

Data Requirements

Use this part of the System Requirements Specification to describe all the input and output data the system must handle. Generally, this data comes from external sources (users and customers included) and must be received or transmitted into and out of the system in a certain format.

For input data, specify each data item and the format in which it will be received. Do the same for all output data.

In addition to customers and users, another source of data requirements are those generated by legacy systems. This can be good and bad. In the case of a well-documented legacy system, it will be an easy matter to specify the data requirements. However, if the legacy system is not well documented, determining the data requirements can take substantially longer to understand.

Finally, in some instances existing data must be reformatted or converted for use by the new system. Data conversion requirements are very important as this task can be expensive and time consuming to complete.

When writing data requirements, keep in mind that more often than not, an element of code will have to be written to handle the data requirement. This could be software that reformats the data coming from a legacy system or code that formats the data coming out of the new system and destined for a legacy system. In any event, this type of design consideration is exactly what one is trying to document when defining the data requirements for the system.

Human Interface Requirements

This section describes the requirements for the Graphical User Interface (GUI) for the system. In some cases it might be easiest to use actual mockups or prototypes of the interface elements to capture the requirements. For example, mockups might include prototypes of web pages.

Human interface requirements can also be specified as data that will be input into the system from users or customers or data that the user or customer must get out of the system. Consider things such as the types of reports the system has to generate (output data), as well as the types of queries needed to generate the required reports.

Security Requirements

When specifying system-level security requirements, be sure to go beyond the obvious. For example, a web-based order entry system is going to be connected to the Internet. Therefore, a key security requirement is protecting the site from hackers. That is the obvious part. But do not think you are done there. Other security requirements might be more complicated, such as protecting credit card information, not only from Internet hackers, but also from employees within the enterprise who have access to the credit card servers.

Security can also include more obtuse parameters, such as protecting source files and the operational system from malicious employees. This can lead to a whole array of unique security requirements that may have gone undocumented.

Another area of security deals with protecting trade secrets. If your enterprise is about to launch, or is thinking about launching, a site that will one-up the competition, there are going to be other security considerations as well.

Remember, when thinking about security, that not all security requirements have to be allocated to software. Some requirements can be allocated to the physical environment, such as keeping servers in locked areas. Other requirements can be allocated to procedures, such as implementing a "need-to-know" policy for all employees on the project.

The upshot on security requirements is that they may entail many requirements that might not be implemented directly by new software. However, these requirements must be captured, so that the total cost for the project can be determined, even though some of this cost might not be directly related to software development.

In summary, security requirements can be allocated to:

❑ The new system software

❑ Operating system security features

❑ Other software security features (e.g. database security)

❑ Physical means (facilities, locked doors etc.)

❑ Policies

❑ Procedures

System State Requirements
System states, also known as modes, can become a fairly in-depth subject, so we will not go into much detail here other than to explain the general concept.

States refer to how the system operates under different conditions. For example, a requirement to transmit data might operate differently when the system is in a test state versus an operational state. Based on this example, the hypothetical system would have two states, a system test state and an operational state.

Knowing this, the analyst would have to define two requirements for transmitting data. For example, in the operational state, data entered by a customer goes to a database. However, in the test state, the data entered might go to analysis software. There are now two requirements for handling output data, one for the operational state and one for the test state.

Approaching requirements with states in mind will lead to a very robust design, but also one that might be significantly more complicated. Keep in mind that specifying the system states is crucial to understanding how the system behaves under different operational scenarios. In some cases, this might be very important, and in others it simply will not matter.

System Interfaces

Nothing is more important than specifying the system interfaces. Do this before anything else. It is a rare system that does not interface with something else, be it a legacy system or some other system that has to be built. Remember, a common cause of cost and schedule overruns is not properly defining the interfaces.

When thinking about interfaces, remember both internal and external interfaces should be covered. Internal interfaces are interfaces between the major components that comprise the new system. External interfaces are interfaces between the new system and legacy systems with which it interacts.

Categories of external interfaces include interfaces with:

❑ Legacy systems

❑ Users

❑ Customers

❑ Other businesses

❑ Hardware devices

❑ Other new systems

"ilities"
So called because these types of requirements end in "ility." They include:

❑ **Reliability** — Refers to requirements focused on guaranteeing that the system works as planned.

❑ **Availability** — Refers to how much time the system is up and operational, for example, 24 hours-a-day, 7 days-a-week, 365 days-a-year.

❑ **Maintainability** — Maintainability refers to the ease of enhancing the system with new functionality as well as correcting defects in the operational system.

❑ **Scalability** — Refers to the fact that the system can expand to handle ever-increasing loads, such as more customers or hits per day.

The "ilities" are difficult to define and test. However, an "ility" such as maintainability is extremely important, as it influences costs over the lifetime of the system. It is not hard to see how it may be possible to spend many times the cost of developing the system maintaining it over many years. Consider your own IT organization. How much of your budget is earmarked for maintaining your current systems? Well-designed systems will be easier to maintain than poorly designed ones.

Notice also that availability and maintainability are related, even though availability is easier to quantify and design for. A 100 percent availability requirement necessitates redundant system design to allow for maintenance or upgrades. Availability requirements also impact hardware selection and can be serious cost drivers.

Other Requirements

When specifying requirements for a new project, one tends to focus entirely on those requirements that will be implemented in software. When an analyst sits down and starts writing requirements, his or her primary focus is on those requirements for which some software must be written. The system analyst, by trade, thinks in terms of databases, web pages, and code.

True system engineering must consider other aspects of the system as well, especially those aspects of the system that will not be implemented with software, but which still might drive overall cost and design considerations.

These requirements include:

❑ Logistics requirements

❑ Personnel requirements

❑ Training requirements

The reasons for considering these types of requirements come down to cost and schedule. Every requirement has to be implemented in some way. Generally speaking, that means every requirement is going to cost something and, in most cases, spending money also means spending time. Therefore, it is safe to say that every requirement has an associated cost and schedule impact, within reason, of course.

Since the Detailed Planning phase is focused on creating an accurate cost and schedule estimate for the project, it is easy to see why it is important to specify non-software related requirements. These requirements will impact the overall budget and schedule, and if the project is going to be completed on time and on budget, non-software related requirements must be budgeted for and scheduled accordingly.

Even though we will not spend a great deal of time dealing with these requirements in this book, do not ignore them on your projects. Giving some thought to these requirements upfront can save you a great deal of time and money later in the project.

Logistics Requirements

Requirements that are not implemented by software still require attention. Good examples are logistics requirements that pertain to delivering the completed system and maintaining it once it becomes operational.

Some readers might object to going into detail on this subject, since it does not really involve building software. That is not the point. Ideally, when talking about requirements at the system level, an analyst should consider all requirements for the simple reason that every requirement costs something to implement. Deciding how the system is going to be fielded and maintained could significantly influence design and budget considerations. Therefore, it is truly imperative that you give this important subject some consideration along with the rest of the system requirements.

Training Requirements

When considering training requirements, consider both maintainer and user training. Maintainer training is often not an issue because some of the developers of the system often hang back and maintain the system after the development effort is complete. These developers will know the system inside-out and generally do not need training.

The more complicated situation arises when the developers will not be the maintainers. In this case, a plan (with its associated costs) must be developed to transition the developers off the program and, at the same time, ramp up the skill base of the maintainers.

A more realistic problem comes from the perspective of user/customer training. When approaching this problem, you should first decide how intuitive the system has to be.

For less obvious functions, several options can be employed, such as providing an explanation as static text on a web page or providing a more conventional "Help" menu button.

More complex forms of training involve developing user manuals and/or conducting training classes. Implementing these forms of training can be very costly and must be identified early, when the total estimate for the project is being prepared.

A Few Last Things

As has been suggested earlier, system requirements are captured and documented in the System Requirements Specification. Since this document is widely used, all rules applicable to writing other types of documents apply. Remember not to forget to include the following in the System Requirements Specification:

❑ Title page

❑ Table of contents

❑ Acronym list

❑ Release date

❑ Release number

❑ Points of contact

Including these items makes the System Requirements Specification much easier to use. Especially important is the inclusion of the release number and date so that developers know they have the most current version of the document.

Requirements are the key to building robust, reliable, and scaleable systems and are crucial for estimating the total cost of the new system accurately. If you always think in terms of covering all the types of requirements that you are likely to encounter with your system and always keep in mind the rules outlined earlier for writing requirements, then you will be halfway there.

Finally, it is very important to control changes to the system requirements document once it is finished. Remember, this document is crucial for estimating the total development cost for the project. If changes to the document are not controlled, the cost estimate will not be accurate.

Typically, once the System Requirements Specification has been written, a formal review is held with all the stakeholders to ensure that the System Requirements Specification meets everyone's expectations. Once the review is completed, the document can be considered baselined. From that point forward, changes must be controlled.

We will discuss how to review and control changes to the System Requirements Specification, as well as other products created on a project, in Chapter 9, "Managing Change," and in Chapter 10, "Managing Quality."

Now that we know how to collect system requirements, the next step is to learn how to use them as a basis for taking the rough cost and schedule estimate created during the Executive Planning phase and converting it to a much more accurate cost and schedule estimate. We will turn our attention to that next.

C H A P T E R   4

Estimating Costs

DURING THE EXECUTIVE PLANNING phase, an organization creates a Statement of Work and a rough estimate of the project's total cost and schedule. Based on these estimates, the organization conducts financial, technical, and schedule feasibility analyses. Depending on the results of these studies, executives will decide whether or not to proceed with the project. If the decision is to fund the project, the next step is to determine and document the system requirements so that a much more accurate estimate of the overall development cost can be generated.

We learned how to collect system requirements in the previous chapter. In this chapter, we will learn how to use the system requirements and the Statement of Work to create a very accurate cost estimate for the project. In the next chapter, we will learn how to convert the estimate into a detailed financial project plan.

Estimating Development Costs

The first step in the estimating process is to estimate development costs. Development costs include tasks like:

❏ Designing

❏ Coding

❏ Prototyping

❏ Testing

They do not include tasks such as training and procurement. Those are estimated later.

If you noticed that development tasks are very similar to the steps of a development life cycle, you are correct. Typically, most of the development tasks are nothing more than software development life cycle steps. This point can be more readily seen by considering the following Statement of Work for a hypothetical project called the "Widget Ordering System":

1.0   **WIDGET ORDERING SYSTEM**
1.1   Analysis
1.2   Top level design
1.3   Detailed design
1.4   Coding
1.5   Testing
1.6   Project management
1.7   Travel
1.8   Software procurement
1.9   Hardware procurement
1.10   Configuration management
1.11   Quality assurance
1.12   Risk management

Based on this Statement of Work, you can see that the project manager chose a life cycle consisting of five steps, namely: Analysis, Top-Level Design, Detailed Design, Coding and Testing. As explained earlier, these life cycle steps are listed in the Statement of Work as tasks that must be completed. They are the development tasks that must be estimated. In this example, the life cycle steps (i.e., the development tasks) appear as the first five tasks in the Statement of Work.

Keep in mind that the methodology we are going to learn does not presuppose any type of life cycle. The methodology works equally well for any type of life cycle, whether it is a Rapid Application Development (RAD), a waterfall, or an iterative life cycle. The only requirement is that the life cycle has a set of steps for which costs can be determined.

Knowing the steps in the life cycle is the first piece of information needed to estimate the development effort. The second piece of information needed is an understanding of the system requirements.

The estimating methodology is based on analyzing the system requirements against the life cycle steps to estimate a cost for each requirement. In other words, if the life cycle consists of three steps, namely Design, Coding, and Testing, then we would look at the requirements and determine how much time it is going to take to create a design that will implement the requirement and also how long it is going to take to code the design and then test the code. If the life cycle contains a prototyping step, then we would estimate how long it would take to create a prototype implementing the requirement.

Although this might seem complicated, it really is not. The following simple example will help make the concept clear.

Assume we have the following set of system requirements:

1.0 *Shall be able to view general ledger entries by date*
2.0 *Shall be able to select consumer accounts*
3.0 *Shall be able to create marketing codes*
4.0 *Shall be able to enter products in a catalog*
5.0 *Shall be able to view general ledger entries by invoice number*
6.0 *Shall be able to select business accounts*
7.0 *Shall be able to change marketing codes*
8.0 *Shall be able to change catalog entries*

In this example, we are only using eight system requirements. Of course, a real set of system requirements would contain hundreds or even thousands of requirements. However, to keep the example understandable, we will use the above eight requirements, which are adequate for this illustration. Regardless of the complexity or number of requirements, the process is the same.

Consider the first requirement, which is:

1.0   Shall be able to view general ledger entries by date.

The first step in our life cycle is Analysis. This step consists of breaking down the system requirements into lower-level requirements that can be handed over to developers for design and coding.

Knowing that, the estimator must determine whether more analysis must be done on the requirements. Remember that the requirements listed above are system requirements and that system requirements are typically at a high level. Generally, system requirements must be broken down into lower-level requirements through functional decomposition or other methodologies, such as Use Cases, before a developer will have enough detail to know exactly what needs to be built.

Looking at the first requirement, the estimator might determine that it will take an additional fifty hours of analysis to define the requirement to the point where there is no ambiguity. At that level, the requirement is defined down to a level low enough that it can be handed over to a developer for implementation.

From the life cycle and the Statement of Work, the development process includes two levels of design, namely, a top-level design effort and a detailed design step. Based on a hypothetical life cycle chosen for this project, the top-level design includes identifying the components and objects required to implement all the requirements and also includes defining the interfaces between those components and objects. The detailed design phase includes determining the inner workings of each component or object.

Considering the first requirement and understanding its relationship to other requirements from a design standpoint, the estimator might determine that the top level and detailed design tasks both require twenty hours of effort to complete.

Knowing the costs in hours of designing objects and components provides information on how much time it will take to code and to test the associated objects. In our example, these might be estimated at forty hours for coding and forty hours for testing.

Summarizing all parts of the estimate for the first requirement leads to the estimate summary shown in Figure 4-1 below:

	Estimate In Hours				
	Complete Analysis	Complete Top Level Design	Complete Detailed Design	Complete Coding	Complete Testing
1 - Shall be able to view general ledger entries by date	50	20	20	40	40

Figure 4-1 Estimate Summary

As shown in Figure 4-1, the total estimated time to implement the first requirement is 170 hours. This includes the time required to complete analysis, create a design, code the design, and, finally, test the code.

When considering the estimate above, several points have to be made.

First, the estimate is only as good as the person making the estimate. Estimates are just that: estimates. Some estimates are better than others. In any case, the estimate is based on professional judgment. Whoever makes the estimate must have enough experience to look at a requirement and, based on past experience, determine how long it should take to implement the requirement. Obviously, if the person doing the estimate has no experience with implementing certain types of requirements, then the estimate will not be very good. Someone who specializes in building order entry systems probably will not be very good at providing estimates for accounting systems.

An estimate's quality can be improved by having multiple people make an estimate or review an estimate. Peer reviews of estimates should be an integral part of any estimating procedure.

In addition, when there is uncertainty pertaining to the estimate, some margin of error must be applied. In other words, estimators must have a degree of confidence in their estimate. If that confidence level is not 100 percent, then the estimate should be padded. This means that an estimate will be increased by some amount or percentage to account for uncertainties. This procedure is called a management reserve.

Second, in order to make an estimate for tasks such as design, related requirements must be considered together. The reason for this is that a design usually implements aspects of many related requirements. One typically does not create a design for a single requirement, and this fact must be reflected in the cost estimate.

For example, if there was just one requirement, it might take twenty hours to come up with a design for that requirement. However, if there are four related requirements, the total design might still take twenty hours, or five hours per requirement. For an actual project, it might be splitting hairs or impossible to determine that one of the four requirements takes five, six, or seven hours to design for, but that is not the point. The important thing is to estimate the total design time for the four related requirements. As you will see later, it is just a matter of convenience to allocate the five hours to each requirement, even though the estimate per requirement might not be totally accurate. This does not matter as long as the total estimate for the four requirements is accurate.

Third, approaching an estimate in this manner implies that some upfront thought has been given to a development task such as design. To estimate the time it will take to design a system, one must have some idea of how it will be designed. Otherwise, how would the estimate be determined?

Common functionality has to be identified and estimated accordingly. For example, if multiple parts of the system make use of a currency feed, then the cost for designing and building that piece of software, with its associated generic interface, has to be estimated. This entails having some idea of the design upfront.

In any case, it is an understanding of the system requirements that makes creating a good object-oriented design possible, and each requirement, even if considered with other requirements, has a percentage of the total cost associated with its implementation.

To return to the example, the complete estimate for the development tasks is shown in Figure 4-2 below.

	Estimate In Hours				
	Complete Analysis	Complete Top Level Design	Complete Design Detailed	Complete Coding	Complete Testing
1 - Shall be able to view general ledger entries by date	50	20	20	40	40
2 - Shall be able to select consumer accounts	40	10	10	30	30
3 - Shall be able to create marketing codes	30	10	10	20	20
4 - Shall be able to enter products in a catalog	30	15	15	20	20
5 - Shall be able to view general ledger entries by invoice number	50	15	15	30	30
6 - Shall be able to select business accounts	60	25	25	40	40
7 - Shall be able to change marketing codes	70	25	25	60	60
8 - Shall be able to change catalog entries	70	40	40	80	80
Total Hours	400	160	160	320	320

Figure 4-2 Total Project Estimate

Figure 4-2 shows that completing the analysis, that is, taking the system requirements and refining them down to a level where they can be turned over to a developer, requires 400 additional hours. Similarly, completing the top-level design requires 160 hours and so on. The total project is estimated to require a total of 1,360 hours, which is the sum of the hours for each phase of the life cycle.

At this point, the total number of hours required to complete the development tasks have been estimated. This estimate is not a project plan and does not include an estimate for non-developmental tasks such as Project Management. Additionally, even for the estimated tasks, we still have not determined important pieces of information such as task durations or dependencies. All that is known is that the estimate to complete the development portion of the project is 1,360 hours.

Note that an important consideration is how to estimate testing times. Testing is a very important and time-consuming aspect in the development process. Since testing can have a large influence on the overall estimate, it is covered in great detail in Chapter 11.

Also keep in mind that the 1,360 hours is not the total cost for the project, just the development cost. The Statement of Work in our example identified other tasks that must also be estimated. We will turn our attention to those next.

Estimating Other Costs

Every task on the Statement of Work must be estimated to determine the total estimate for project completion. The following non-development tasks are also listed on the example Statement of Work and must be estimated:

1.6   Project management

1.7   Travel

1.8   Software procurement

1.9   Hardware procurement

1.10 Configuration Management

1.11 Quality Assurance

1.12 Risk management

Next, we will learn how to estimate these tasks.

Estimating Project Management Hours
When estimating how much effort is required to manage a project, two factors must be considered. First, what is the total duration of the development effort, and second, what percentage of a project manager's time is required to manage the project?

To answer the first question, assume that the schedule for a new project indicates that the project will be done in six months. Based on this information, it is easy to calculate how many hours are needed for Project Management.

Before we make the calculation, realize that a typical work year consists of approximately 2,080 hours. This is based on 52 weeks in a year times 40 hours per week, which equals 2,080 hours.

Depending on your company and your company's accounting calendar, realize that most employees actually work about 1,800 hours a year. This is based on subtracting vacations, holidays, and sick time from the total available work hours. Therefore, whether you use 2,080 hours, 1,800 hours per year, or some other number, is up to you and is based on your company's policies.

For our example, assume the greater number of hours, which is 2,080 hours. If the project is six months long, then the project manager will manage the effort for six months, which is half a year. We already said that a year consists of 2,080 hours, so half of that is 1,040 hours. This is the estimate for the project manager.

There is also the question of what percentage of time the project manager needs to spend on the project. In the calculations above, it is assumed that the project manager will manage the effort full time. This might not be the case. The project might be fairly straightforward, requiring that the project manager only spend half of his or her time managing it. In that case, the estimate for the project manager's time would be 520 hours (1,040 hours divided by 2, or 520 hours).

On small-to medium-sized projects, there is typically one project manager overseeing the entire development effort. That person's time could be full or part-time. On more complex efforts, there may be several project managers overseeing different aspects of the development effort. In this case, an estimate for each project manager's time is needed.

A key consideration in determining the project manager's time is knowing the duration of the project. From a simplified standpoint, the duration of the project is calculated by dividing the estimated number of hours for the project by the number of people working on the project. In the next chapter, you will learn how to calculate a project's duration based on the concept of a time-phased resource load.

Estimating Travel Costs

Estimating travel costs requires that the estimator must know the following:

❑ Number of trips

❑ Number of people making the trip

❑ Duration of the trip

❑ Cost of travel

❑ Cost of lodging

❏ Cost of meals

❏ Miscellaneous costs

Of the required information, the number of trips and the number of people traveling per trip are the most important. If either piece of information is incorrect, the total estimate will be incorrect.

A very good way to estimate travel cost is to review previous travel expense reports to get an idea of the cost associated with a typical trip. Based on this historical information, accurate travel cost can be estimated.

Estimating Procurement Costs

Procurement costs generally include both hardware and software procurement. Software procurement typically includes licenses for development software and other licensed products such as database servers.

A key aspect of the Detailed Planning phase, covered in the next chapter, is using the total estimated number of hours for the project and determining the number of developers needed to finish the project by a certain end date. The number of developers on the project, and when the developers roll onto and off of the project, is the key information needed to estimate software procurement (cost for licenses) costs. Determining the total headcount for the project and when those personnel are needed is covered in the next chapter, so we will not go into those details here.

Estimating hardware procurement costs usually revolves around estimating the number of development, test and production workstations, and servers. When estimating server costs, it is important to remember that many companies use three different sets of servers for project work. Typically, the first set of servers is for hosting developmental software, the second set of servers replicates the operational environment and is used for testing, and the third set of hardware is used for the actual production system.

When estimating hardware costs, it is important to know what hardware already exists and what has to be procured. It is also important to know whether a separate test suite of hardware is required.

Estimating Configuration Management Costs

Configuration Management costs are hard to estimate on most projects. When estimating Configuration Management costs, consider the following factors:

Quality and completeness of the system requirements — If the system requirements are well defined, there will be fewer changes than if the requirements are poorly defined. However, even with a well-defined set of system requirements, there will still be changes. Therefore, if the system requirements are not well defined, the Configuration Management estimate will be higher.

Complexity of the project — As the complexity of a project increases, the number of changes will increase proportionately. This is a direct result of the fact that as the project's complexity increases, there will be more functionality that has to change as the project takes shape. Obviously, a simple website type of project can be thought out pretty well prior to the start of the project, minimizing the number of changes occurring after the project starts. This is not the case on complex projects. Complex projects require a higher estimate for Configuration Management than simpler projects.

Complexity of the Configuration Management system — Configuration Management is covered in detail in a later chapter, but some Configuration Management systems are more complex than others. The bottom line is that the more complex the Configuration Management system is, the higher the estimate for its implementation will be.

Criticality of the system — A highly critical software system requires a more robust development methodology. Part of this methodology is the Configuration Management system. The estimate for implementing Configuration Management on a mission critical system will be significantly higher than the estimate for the same Configuration Management system on an intranet system used to post job openings.

Chapter 9, "Managing Change," takes a much deeper look into the subject of Configuration Management. This subject is important because Configuration Management is important for controlling changes and, ultimately, controlling both the cost and schedule baselines. After reading Chapter 9, you will be much better prepared to estimate Configuration Management costs.

Estimating Quality Assurance Costs

As is the case with Configuration Management, estimating Quality Assurance cost varies depending on the complexity of the project and the degree of rigor expected from the Quality Assurance organization. We will take a much deeper look into Quality Assurance in Chapter 10, "Managing Quality." Once you have a good idea of the components that go into a good Quality Assurance program, you will have an easier time estimating this task.

Estimating Risk Management Costs

Risk Management is an ongoing effort throughout the life cycle of the project. This is true because the things that were risky at the beginning of the project are usually not the things that are risky at the end of the project. Since activities occur throughout the development life cycle, it is imperative that the estimate includes hours that can be spread from the beginning of the project until its completion.

When estimating the cost of a program, remember that the estimate must include the following tasks:

❏ Identifying the risk

❏ Qualifying and quantifying the risk

❏ Creating and maintaining a risk abatement plan

Creating a Management Reserve

A management reserve is extra budget, above the estimate, used to cover estimating mistakes. There is always some ambiguity involved in estimating, which makes having a management reserve important. Estimates can be high or low depending on who makes the estimate and how much information is known about the project.

Since estimates are rarely one hundred percent accurate, many organizations create a management reserve in the estimate. The reserve is used to pad the estimate so that the project does not come in higher than the estimate.

How much pad to put into the estimate is primarily driven by the accuracy and fidelity of the system requirements. If the system requirements are incomplete or vague, a higher reserve should be included than if the requirements are clear and detailed.

Another factor dictating the size of the reserve is the familiarity of the estimator and the development team with building a particular type of project. If the new system is an order entry system and the team has done similar projects in the past, then the estimate can be more conservative than if the team has no previous history of building an order entry system.

Once a sense of the relative magnitude of the reserve is established, then the next question becomes where to put it. In this regard there are two possibilities.

One approach is to include a pad on each element of the estimate, making the overall estimate higher than without the reserve. The problem with this approach is that the reserve is buried in the estimate and the relative magnitude is impossible to discern after the estimate is completed. Additionally, this approach misleads project managers as to the true cost and schedule targets they should be managing to, which should be the estimate without the reserve.

A second approach is to estimate the project without the reserve and then to include a separate line item in the estimate for the reserve. This approach has the advantage of clearly showing what the actual reserve is, but makes it susceptible to management elimination.

Regardless of how a reserve is handled, one should be included in every estimate. The actual size of the estimate is based on previous history. If the development organization has a history of completing projects within ten percent of the estimate, then ten percent might be a good reserve. On the other hand, if projects typically come in many percentage points over the estimate, then a higher reserve should definitely be used.

Finally, as you will see in Chapter 9, "Managing Change," the reserve should not be based on expected changes to the scope of the project, such as the addition of new system functionality after the project begins. Scope changes are estimated when they occur and are independent of the management reserve.

With the knowledge of how to create an accurate project estimate that includes both development and non-development tasks, the next step in the Detailed Planning phase is to convert the estimate to a budget and a financial project plan. We will learn how to do that in the next chapter.

CHAPTER 5

Determining the Budget

IN THE PREVIOUS CHAPTER, we learned how to develop an accurate project estimate. Despite the accuracy, there are three issues with this estimate. First, the estimate is in hours (except for things like procurement and travel expenses, which are in dollars). Second, we do not know how many people it will take to complete the project. Third, the hours and people are not time-phased. In other words, we do not know when, in the course of the project, the hours are spent.

In this chapter, we tackle those issues by learning how to convert the hour estimate into an equivalent number of people (hereafter, we will refer to people working on the project as resources) and a budget. Additionally, we will learn how to time phase both the resources and budget across the duration of the project so that we have a complete financial plan from which to manage the project.

Determining the Resource Load

In the following discussions, assume an employee works 160 hours per month. Using an estimate of 160 hours is one approach that works well, but if more accuracy is needed, use your company's accounting calendar. An accounting calendar contains the actual hours of work for each month and takes into account factors such as holidays. Additionally, on longer projects, consider employee vacations and sick time. As mentioned previously, a typical work year contains 2,080 hours (52 weeks times 40 hours per week), but a good rule of thumb is to use 1,800 hours. In other words, a typical employee will work about 1,800 hours in a year after vacation time, sick leave and holidays are considered. All the examples that follow assume a 160 hour work month.

Suppose we had the following simple Statement of Work for a new project:

1.0 WIDGET ORDERING SYSTEM
1.1 Complete analysis
1.2 Top level design
1.3 Detailed design
1.4 Coding
1.5 Testing

Of course, on an actual project, the Statement of Work would include many other tasks, such as Project Management, Quality Assurance, and Configuration Management. In this example, we will ignore these other tasks in order to keep the example simple. Regardless of the number of tasks on the Statement of Work, the process outlined below remains the same.

In addition to the Statement of Work for our new project, also assume that we have the following system requirements (the same ones used in the previous chapter):

1 — Shall be able to view general ledger entries by date
2 — Shall be able to select consumer accounts
3 — Shall be able to create marketing codes
4 — Shall be able to enter products in a catalog
5 — Shall be able to view general ledger entries by invoice number
6 — Shall be able to select business accounts
7 — Shall be able to change marketing codes
8 — Shall be able to change catalog entries

For these requirements, we would create an estimate like the one shown below in Figure 5-1.

	Estimate In Hours				
	Complete Analysis	Complete Top Level Design	Complete Design Detailed	Complete Coding	Complete Testing
1 - Shall be able to view general ledger entries by date	50	20	20	40	40
2 - Shall be able to select consumer accounts	40	10	10	30	30
3 - Shall be able to create marketing codes	30	10	10	20	20
4 - Shall be able to enter products in a catalog	30	15	15	20	20
5 - Shall be able to view general ledger entries by invoice number	50	15	15	30	30
6 - Shall be able to select business accounts	60	25	25	40	40
7 - Shall be able to change marketing codes	70	25	25	60	60
8 - Shall be able to change catalog entries	70	40	40	80	80
Total Hours	**400**	**160**	**160**	**320**	**320**

Figure 5-1 Project Estimate

Combining the task estimates with the Statement of Work, we see the entire development budget for the project in hours. This is shown below in Figure 5-2.

SOW Tasks	Task Hours	Total Hours
1.0 Widget Ordering System		1360
1.1 Complete analysis	400	
1.2 Top level design	160	
1.4 Detailed design	160	
1.5 Coding	320	
1.6 Testing	320	

Figure 5-2 Project Hours by Task

Once an estimate in hours for each task has been determined, the next step is determining the resources necessary to complete the tasks.

Some readers might object to this approach, arguing correctly that a task can really take different lengths of time depending on who does the work. A senior employee could complete a complicated task in 100 hours, but it might take a junior employee 200 hours to finish it. This is a valid point and is surely a consideration. The reality is that when estimating hours for a project, the hours should reflect the expected skill level of the personnel assigned to the task. In other words, if you expect to staff the task with junior employees, then make a higher estimate. On the other hand, if you expect to staff the project with a senior resource, lower the estimate.

Going back to the example, the first Statement of Work task is to complete the analysis phase of the project, which was estimated at 400 hours. Assuming a typical work month of 160 hours, we can do a simple calculation and determine that if one person is assigned to the task, it will take 2.5 months to complete (160 hours + 160 hours + 80 hours = 400 hours).

Alternatively, if it is determined that the task needs to be completed sooner, it might be better to assign two and a half people to the task and complete it in one month. Remember, one person can work 160 hours, so two will spend 360 hours a month. The half person means someone is working half time on the task and this part of the effort equals 80 hours.

Of course, for any number of reasons, it is not always possible to add employees to complete tasks sooner. The optimum number of workers assigned to a task is based on a number of factors, such as employee availability, the nature of the task, and how soon the task must be completed to support the project's end date. All of these factors must be considered carefully when determining the resource mix for a task. In our case, assume we can assign two and a half employees to the task and complete it in one month.

To complete the resource load, we must do the same thing for the remaining tasks. For example, we might assign one person to complete the top-level design, the next task on the Statement of Work, which gives a task duration of one month. Similarly, assigning one person to the detailed design task would also give a duration of one month.

When we complete the resource loading described above, we end up with the resource plan shown in Figure 5-3.

As mentioned above, the number of resources is based on the availability of resources, when the task must be completed and

Statement of Work Task	Estimate in Hours	Number of Resources	Duration in Months
Complete analysis	400	2.5	1
Top level design	160	1	1
Detailed design	160	1	1
Coding	320	2	1
Testing	320	2	1

Figure 5-3 Resource Load

other practical considerations such as how many resources can truly be assigned to the task while maintaining productivity.

Creating the Budget

After the correct number of resources has been determined, the next step is to determine the budget for each task. Budget is based on two factors, namely the number of hours to complete a task and the hourly rate of the employees doing the tasks.

The components of the hourly rate vary from company to company. For example, an hourly rate might be based on the employee's salary plus benefits divided by the number of hours in a year (typically 2,080). Senior employees normally have higher salaries and consequently have a higher hourly rate than more junior employees.

Other costs might be associated with the employee, such as the cost of facilities (the buildings the employees work in) divided by the total number of employees using those facilities. Getting the correct hourly rate for an employee is something your accounting department can help with.

In our example, to keep the arithmetic simple, we will assume that the employees doing the work have salaries equal to $50.00 per hour. Based on that rate, the total budget, in dollars, for each task is shown in Figure 5-4.

Figure 5-4 shows that completing the Analysis task will cost $20,000 dollars. This amount is based on the 400-hour estimate for the task multiplied by the $50.00 per hour rate. Further, if we add up the costs for all tasks on our simple Statement of Work, the total budget for the project is $68,000.

Additionally, we see from Figure 5-4 that it will take five months of effort to finish the project. However, at this point, we do not know whether the five months means that it will actually take five months to complete or some time period less than that. The

Statement of Work Task	Estimate in Hours	Number of Resources	Duration in Months	Budget
Complete analysis	400	2.5	1	$20,000
Top level design	160	1	1	$8,000
Detailed design	160	1	1	$16,000
Coding	320	2	1	$16,000
Testing	320	2	1	$16,000
TOTAL				$68,000

Figure 5-4 The Project's Budge

project could actually be shorter in duration because some tasks may overlap. At this point in the process, the schedule relationships between the tasks have not been determined.

To summarize: first, we created an hours estimate for the project based directly on what had to be built; that is, the estimate was based directly on the system requirements. Next, based on the hours estimate, we determined what resources were needed to complete the project. The resource calculation was based directly on the number of hours in the estimate. Finally, based on the resource plan, we created a budget. The budget calculation was based on the number of hours for a task times the cost of the resource completing the task.

Using this approach, everything we have done so far ties directly together. In other words, the project's estimated cost to build the system is based on the system requirements. Additionally, the budget, in dollars, is tied directly to the hours estimate. Also, the project's budget is tied directly to the rates and numbers of developers building the new system.

Creating the Time-Phased Resource Load

From Figure 5-4, one can gather three important pieces of information. First, we know what the tasks are: analysis, top-level design, detailed design, coding, and testing. Second, we know the duration of each task. Third, we know how much it is going to cost to complete these tasks. Using the first two pieces of information, we can create the time-phased resource load. This not only shows how many resources are being used for each task, but also when those resources are needed.

For our example, the time-phased resource load might look like the one shown in Figure 5-5.

	Month 1	Month 2	Month 3	Month 4	Month 5
Analysis	2.5 EP				
Top level design		1 EP			
Detailed design			1 EP		
Code				2 EP	
Testing					2 EP
TOTAL	2.5 EP	1 EP	1 EP	2 EP	2 EP

Figure 5-5 Time Phased Resource Load

In the Figure 5-5, the acronym EP stands for Equivalent Personnel. One EP is equal to one person working full-time for one month on the task. Similarly, 2.5 EP is two full time people working on the task for the month, plus one person working half time.

How do we know this is what the time-phased resource load looks like? The answer is as follows. We know the analysis phase of the project was estimated at 400 hours. We also know that it was decided that two and a half people could be assigned to this task. This means that the task would take one month to complete and that two and a half people would be involved with the task during that month. Using Figure 5-4, we know the same information for the remaining task.

As you can see, the time-phased resource load is actually a schedule. Consequently, project planners must have some idea of the relationship between tasks before the time-phased resource load can be created. For example, can the preliminary design start before the analysis task is complete or can it only be started after the analysis task has been completed? These are the types of questions answered with a schedule. We know the duration of the tasks from Figure 5-4, but we need to create a schedule to show the relationship between the tasks. Once the schedule is complete, we can create the time-phased resource load because we know how many people are associated with each task on the schedule.

Our example is very simple, especially as to the relationship between the tasks. On actual projects, one would create a schedule to determine when tasks start and stop and to show the relationship between the tasks. We will learn how to create schedules in Chapter 7, "Scheduling." For now, to keep the example simple and to emphasize the process, we can assume that there is a sequential relationship between tasks and that the top-level design starts after analysis. We must recognize that when it comes to actual projects, tasks overlap, and their relationship to each other can be very complicated.

The time-phased resource load is important because it shows when personnel are rolling onto and off of the project. It can be used for determining how many desks, licenses, and so on are needed for the project. It is also needed to create the time-phased budget, which is covered next.

Creating the Time-Phased Budget

A time-phased budget is exactly what the name implies. It is the total budget for the project spread out across the duration of the project. The time-phased budget is based on the time-phased resource load and for our simple example looks like the one shown in Figure 5-6.

	Month 1	Month 2	Month 3	Month 4	Month 5
Complete Analysis	$20,000				
Preliminary design		$8,000			
Detailed design			$8,000		
Code				$16,000	
Testing					$16,000
TOTAL	$20,000	$8,000	$8,000	$16,000	$16,000

Figure 5-6 Time Phased Resource Load

How do we know this is what the time-phased budget looks like? The answer is that the time-phased budget is based directly on the time-phased resource load. In other words, we know that completing the analysis phase was estimated at 400 hours. We also know that it was decided that two and a half people could be assigned this task. This means that the task would take one month to complete.

We also know that the salaries for the employees completing the analysis would be $20,000 based on the duration of the task, namely 400 hours, and the fact that these employees cost $50.00 per hour.

We can complete a similar type of analysis for each task, and then knowing how the tasks relate to each other, we can create the time-phased budget shown above.

When looking at the time-phased budget, notice that reading it horizontally shows how the budget is allocated per month for each task. Reading vertically shows the total budget for a month and what tasks are being worked on during that month.

Regardless of how tasks overlap, the principles for creating the time-phased budget are the same, it is just that the real-world application of these principles becomes more complicated.

Now that we know how to create the time-phased resource load and time-phased budget, the next step is to learn how to allocate the budget to the organizational elements that will actually do the work. In order to manage a project, we not only need a budget, but we also have to create a development organization to do the work. Each element of that organization must have a piece of the budget corresponding to their piece of the work. We cover how to do that next.

CHAPTER 6

Determining the Development Organization and Allocating Budget

IN PREVIOUS CHAPTERS, we showed how to use the system requirements to define and quantify what a new system must accomplish for the business. We also showed how to use the Statement of Work and the system requirements to estimate the project's total cost in hours. In the last chapter, we learned how to convert the estimate into a time-phased resource load and a time-phased budget.

Once a budget (in either dollars or hours) has been determined, it must be allocated to the organization elements actually doing the work. For example, if a large project includes an accounting piece, an order entry part, and a supply chain management piece, the budget must be allocated to the group developing the accounting piece as well as the groups completing the other parts of the new system. Developing the accounting piece has an associated budget and resource load, and this must be allocated to the project manager responsible for developing this piece.

Of course, before the budget can be allocated, there must be a development organization to which it can be allocated. In this chapter, we will focus on techniques you can use to determine the optimum development organization for a new project. Keep in mind that large projects often require complicated organizations. This is because a large project might involve a hundred or more developers and support personnel. A project of this size requires one or more project managers and multiple leads. Therefore, our next step is to learn how to create an organization that can actually build the software and then learn how to allocate a budget to each element of that organization. Before we get down to specifics, we must first talk a little bit about the parts that comprise a software system.

Defining a System

A system, as defined here, is a collection of software that performs a bounded set of functionality. By bounded, we mean a well-defined set of functionality that is formally documented. This functionality meets business, scientific, or other objectives of an enterprise or an organization within an enterprise.

A strict definition of a system includes not only the new software under development, but also hardware and off-the-shelf software such as database systems and operating systems. In many instances a system might include legacy software such as an old accounting system built ten years ago.

Since a system includes a large set of varied functionality, it is often useful to break it down into components called subsystems. For example, a very large system might include an Accounting subsystem and an Order Entry subsystem. The Accounting subsystem would include traditional accounting functions such as Accounts Receivable, Accounts Payable, General Ledger, and perhaps related functions such as Finance and Planning.

From a Project Management standpoint, the reason for breaking a system down into subsystems is to make management of the total development effort easier. For example, all the software on an

Air Force aircraft can be considered one system consisting of sub-systems such as the Guidance, Navigation, Flight Control, and Weapons Control subsystems. If you were in charge of develop-ing this very complex system, you would assign different develop-ment teams to each subsystem. You could have a team assigned to develop the aircraft's Guidance, Navigation, and Flight Con-trol subsystems, and another team responsible for developing the aircraft's Weapons Control subsystem.

When approaching a complex development effort in this manner, you should assign each team complete responsibility for building and testing their subsystem. If done correctly, and if the interfaces between the subsystems are correct, the different teams can de-velop their subsystems independently of each other, and then, at the end of the project, hook the subsystems together. The Guid-ance, Navigation, and Flight Control subsystems should interface correctly with the Weapons Control subsystem and with each other.

This idea of breaking a system down into subsystems for manage-ment purposes can be taken a step further. Each subsystem can also have its own development schedule, budget, and project de-liverables.

This technique works well as long as each subsystem's schedule and budget "trees up" correctly to the system's schedule and bud-get. We will discuss this in more detail later, but first let us turn our attention to some criteria that help in determining the subsys-tems within a system.

How to Determine Subsystems

Some of the more common criteria for determining a subsystem are:

❑ Functional similarities

❑ Hardware similarities

Let us take a look at each.

Functional Similarities

A good example of functional similarity is found in the business units associated with the system. For example, all functionality related to the warehouse aspects of the business might be considered a subsystem while another subsystem might be all software supporting the financial aspects of the business. Functional similarities are the most common criteria for determining subsystems.

When determining functional similarities, the system requirements are used. Grouping the system requirements by related functionality will provide the planner with a very good idea of what the subsystems are. For instance, in the example above, it would be very easy to determine which system requirements pertain to the warehousing aspects of the project versus which requirements pertain to the financial aspects of the system. Even a cursory look at the system requirements should leave little doubt about how to split a system into subsystems based on functional similarities.

Sometimes a group of functions are related in other ways. A client/server application is a good example. The most obvious approach might be to make all the software and hardware related to the server portion of the system one subsystem and all the hardware and software related to the client portion another subsystem.

Yet another aspect of functional similarity results from unique and related requirements. For example, parts of the system that have similar security requirements might be grouped together as a subsystem, or parts of the system that have unique logistics considerations, such as upgrades or operator training, might be grouped together as a subsystem.

Hardware Similarities

Hardware considerations also form a basis for determining subsystems. In the client/server example, it may be determined that a large portion of the software runs on a high-end server or maybe even on a mainframe, making this software an obvious subsystem choice. If a large chunk of the software runs on PCs, that software might be an obvious choice for a subsystem.

On very large systems like a Department of Defense weapon system, hardware platforms are extremely important for determining subsystems. For example, all the avionics and flight control software on an aircraft may be considered part of an airborne subsystem and the ground-based command and control portions might be considered another subsystem.

Software Configuration Items

For a complicated system, subsystems are too large and complex to be easily developed and managed. In the event of very large or complex subsystems, the management effort is significantly simplified by breaking subsystems down into smaller pieces called Configuration Items (CIs). A CI is a logical grouping of software components or objects. In this discussion, we are not down to the component or object (for example, a Java class) level yet. Rather, Configuration Items consist of software objects and components.

As in the case with subsystems, there are general attributes associated with CIs. These are:

❏ CIs contain a related group of functionality

❏ CIs have their own set of documentation

❏ CIs have their own formal reviews

❏ CIs are developed by a single team

❏ CIs have their own budget

❏ CIs have their own schedule

The first attribute is self-explanatory. This is the main criterion for grouping a set of functions as a CI.

Again, the system requirements are used to determine Configuration Items but instead of looking at the complete set of system requirements as was necessary to determine the subsystems, the planner only considers the system requirements allocated to a subsystem in order to determine the CIs for that subsystem.

The second attribute deals with documentation. In most cases, a CI will have its own Software Requirements Specification, design document, and test plan. This makes keeping control of the CI simpler and makes managing and testing the CI more straightforward.

The fact that a CI has its own set of documentation leads naturally to the third attribute, indicating that a CI also has its own set of formal reviews. This is the case since most formal documentation, such as a requirements specification, is formally reviewed by business owners for approval. Since CIs have their own documentation, they also have reviews that go with that documentation. Reviews include:

❑ Software requirements reviews

❑ Design reviews

❑ Code reviews

❑ Test reviews

One of the most significant (from a management standpoint) attributes of a CI is the fact that a unique team can be assigned to develop it. Since a CI is a fairly large block of software, and since a CI consists of a tightly related set of functionality, it makes sense to assign a unique team with the responsibility for its development. This does not mean that the team members developing one CI cannot also be involved with other CIs. It just means that CIs are well enough defined that they can be turned over to a team for implementation.

Since a unique team is involved in developing a CI, a discreet budget can be given to the team. This is the second-to-the-last attribute listed above. Of course, associated with that budget there is also a unique schedule.

Software Components and Objects

Just as subsystems are composed of CIs, CIs are composed of lower-level software components and objects. Obviously, one type of component is an object consisting of a related group of functions and data similar to a C++ or Java class. Other components might be web pages or database objects. Several competing technologies and approaches exist for defining and building objects, but that is not important to this discussion. Whichever technology or approach is chosen, the concept is the same; a CI is composed of a group of components or objects that implement a related set of functionality.

Subsystems Versus Configuration Items

For smaller to midsize projects, it is often advantageous to skip the concept of a subsystem and instead define the system in terms of a set of Configuration Items. In other words, the system is defined entirely by CIs.

Using the concept of a subsystem does not make sense in the case of a small system that has two major blocks of functionality. For a simple system such as this, it would be better to assume that the system is comprised of two Configuration Items and leave it at that. As you will see, the process of allocating a budget is the same regardless of whether subsystems, Configuration Items, or both are used.

Hardware Configuration Items

At this point we need to change subjects and move from talking about software to talking briefly about hardware. We are not going to concern ourselves too much with hardware, but we need to discuss a few aspects of it to get a complete understanding of everything that has to go into the Detailed Planning phase of a large effort. Like Software Configuration Items, Hardware Configuration Items (HCIs) are hardware items such as servers, routers, and even cables. All Software Configuration Items run on a Hardware Configuration Item.

Typical examples of Hardware Configuration Items include the web server, the database server, and the application server. Other examples of Hardware Configuration Items include firewalls, routers, switches, and bridges.

The complete list of hardware required to develop, test, and field the system is collected in a document called the Hardware Utilization List (HUL). The HUL is used for planning, budgeting, and scheduling purposes and is written during the Detailed Planning phase of a new project.

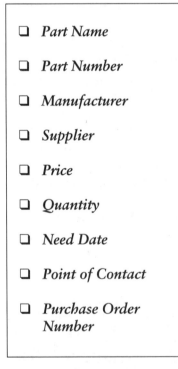

❑ *Part Name*

❑ *Part Number*

❑ *Manufacturer*

❑ *Supplier*

❑ *Price*

❑ *Quantity*

❑ *Need Date*

❑ *Point of Contact*

❑ *Purchase Order Number*

Figure 6-1
Information in a HUL

Figure 6-1 lists the key components of a HUL. As shown in the figure, the HUL is nothing more than a list of information about each Hardware Configuration Item. This information makes procuring the hardware straightforward, especially when a group other than the IT organization does the procurement.

A key piece of information to include on any HUL is the "need date" for each Hardware Configuration Item. Knowing the need date ensures that long lead items are procured in a timely manner. It also ensures that valuable resources are not spent procuring hardware that is not needed until late in the development effort.

It is important to include all Hardware Configuration Items on the HUL. It is especially important to include all hardware required for redundancy and testing.

It is also important to identify Hardware Configuration Items up front since all of the Software Configuration Items must be allocated to HCIs. Once this allocation is complete, performance issues can be addressed and verified. In this regard, do not forget to include any legacy hardware used with the new system. Identification of this hardware is particularly important, as it may be the weak link in the overall performance of the new system.

Now that we know about systems, subsystems, and software and Hardware Configuration Items, we can learn how to allocate budget to the organizational elements that are going to build those subsystems and Configuration Items. The easiest way to understand this is with a simple example.

Allocating Budget

Allocating budget to the organizational elements that will do the work is a four-step process. The steps are:

❑ **Step 1** — Define the system

❑ **Step 2** — Determine the development organization

❑ **Step 3** — Allocate budget

❑ **Step 4** — Allocate schedule

Consider the following illustration of these steps.

Step 1 — Define the System

Suppose senior executives at company X want to automate, through a new software system, all the basic elements of their business. The business elements for company X include accounting, order entry, fulfillment, and marketing. The executives decide to call the new system the *Enterprise Management System.*

During the Detailed Planning phase for the Enterprise Management System, the following system requirements are gathered (same ones used previously):

1. *Shall be able to view general ledger entries by date*
2. *Shall be able to select consumer accounts*
3. *Shall be able to create marketing codes*
4. *Shall be able to enter products into a catalog*
5. *Shall be able to view general ledger entries*
   by invoice number
6. *Shall be able to select business accounts*
7. *Shall be able to change marketing codes*
8. *Shall be able to change catalog entries*

To keep the example simple, there are only eight system requirements. As we mentioned in the previous chapter, on an actual project the number of system requirements would be in the hundreds if not thousands. Regardless of the actual number of system requirements, the process is the same.

When looking at the system requirements, you will see that there are basically four distinct types of requirements that have been gathered. For example, two of the system requirements (i.e., requirements 1 and 5) clearly deal with accounting functions, while the others deal with marketing, order entry, and fulfillment.

Using this information, we can take the original set of system requirements and group them as follows:

Accounting Requirements
Shall be able to view general ledger entries by date
Shall be able to view general ledger entries by invoice number

Order Entry Requirements
Shall be able to select consumer accounts
Shall be able to select business accounts

Marketing Requirements
Shall be able to create marketing codes
Shall be able to change marketing codes

Fulfillment Requirements
Shall be able to enter products into a catalog
Shall be able to change catalog entries

Based on how we grouped the requirements, we can *define* our system as shown in Figure 6-2.

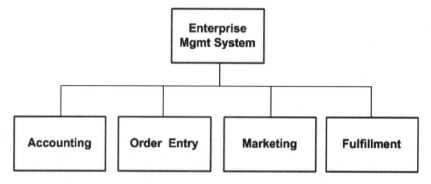

Figure 6-2 Enterprise Managment System

In this example, Accounting, Order Entry, Marketing, and Fulfillment are the major blocks of functionality. Due to their size, they represent the four major subsystems in the Enterprise Management System. Figure 6-2 represents the first part of the system definition. At this point we do not know what the Configuration Items are, but for now that is not important. What is important is knowing how to use the system definition shown above to:

❑ Determine the organization for the project

❑ Allocate budget to the organizational elements of the project

❑ Allocate schedule to the organizational elements of the project

Step 2 — Determine the Development Organization

Every project requires a development organization to implement the project. Typically, this includes developers and a project manager. Of course, there are also specialists on the project such as system architects, Configuration Management experts, Quality Assurance personnel, and testers.

The larger the project, the more complex the organization becomes. This is where the definition of a system is very helpful.

To use a generally accepted term, a *Program Manager* is someone who manages project managers. Based on this definition, we can assign the following types of personnel to the levels of the project:

System — Program Manager
Subsystem — Project Manager
Configuration Item — Project Manager or Lead
Components/Objects — Developers

What this means is that if one has a system consisting of subsystems, it will more than likely have an organization consisting of a Program Manager, project managers, leads, and developers. An organization for the example project above is shown in Figure 6-3.

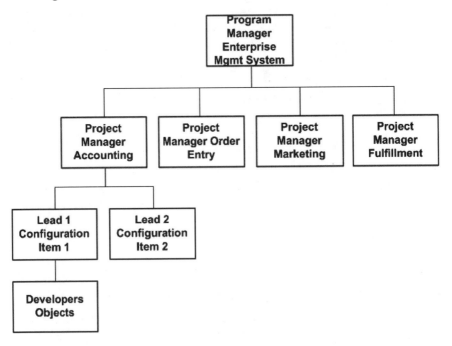

Figure 6-3 Organization for the Enterprise Management System

Some readers might consider this organization somewhat bureaucratic, but consider the following rationale.

A subsystem was defined as major blocks of functionality. Certainly the accounting piece falls into this category. Within the Accounting subsystem there are Configuration Items. These might include accounts receivable, accounts payable, and the general ledger functionality. Each of the Configuration Items requires a fairly significant team for development. For example, depending on the complexity, the general ledger Configuration Item might require four or five people to implement it. This many developers require some management, and as we pointed out above, this level of management would be a lead. For the accounting piece alone, we might have three or four leads. Managing a team of this size requires a project manager. Of course, one project manager might manage several smaller subsystems.

When considering the management requirements for an organization such as the one shown above, keep the following in mind. Moving from the top of the organization chart to the bottom implies decreasing management responsibilities and increasing technical responsibilities. For instance, in our example, the top position in the organization is the Program Manager. This person would spend close to 100 percent of his/her time on management concerns and very little time on technical issues.

Moving lower in the organization, project managers still spend a great deal of their time on management issues but would also spend some percentage of their time on technical issues more so than would the Program Manager.

A lead, on the other hand, would be managing a group of five or six developers and would be required to be heavily involved in the technical aspects of the project with minimal time devoted to management issues.

Developers, of course, would be fully involved with technical issues and not be overly concerned with management issues.

Step 3 — Allocate Budget

Once the system has been defined and an organization put together to build the new system, the next step is to allocate a budget to the organizational elements responsible for building each part of the new system. In our example, the organizational elements are subsystems. Each subsystem has a project manager assigned to it, and so each project manager should have a budget to build his or her piece.

Continuing with our example, suppose our eight requirements, now sorted by subsystems, were estimated as shown in Figure 6-4.

Figure 6-4 shows that of the total 1,360 hours estimated to complete the project, the Accounting subsystem project manager is responsible for 310 hours, the Order Entry Project subsystem project manager is responsible for 310 hours, and so on.

In other words the Accounting project manager must manage the accounting development effort so that it is completed within the estimated 310 hours. Keep in mind that this is a very simple example and that, in reality, the accounting effort might include hundreds of requirements and an estimate to complete the project in thousands of hours, not hundreds. Regardless of the size of the project, the principle is the same.

The key point is that this approach ties the budget that is allocated to a development group directly to the original estimate and budget.

Step 4 — Allocate Schedule

In the previous chapter, we briefly discussed how to estimate the schedule for each task based on the total budget for the task divided by the number of resources assigned to the task. We can extend that concept to include organizational elements doing the work.

Assume, for a minute, that the Accounting subsystem was estimated at 4,160 hours (not the 310 hours used in the above example) to complete. The 4,160 hours means that two people can

	ESTIMATE IN HOURS					
	Complete Analysis	Complete Top Level Design	Complete Detailed Design	Complete Coding	Complete Testing	Total
1 - Shall be able to view general ledger entries by date	50	20	20	40	40	
5 - Shall be able to view general ledger entries by invoice number	50	15	15	30	30	
Total Accounting	**100**	**35**	**35**	**70**	**70**	**310**
2 - Shall be able to select consumer accounts	40	10	10	30	30	
6 - Shall be able to select business accounts	60	25	25	40	40	
Total Order Entry	**100**	**35**	**35**	**70**	**70**	**310**
3 - Shall be able to create marketing codes	30	10	10	20	20	
7 - Shall be able to change marketing codes	70	25	25	60	60	
Total Marketing	**100**	**35**	**35**	**80**	**80**	**330**
4 - Shall be able to enter products in a catalog	30	15	15	20	20	
8 - Shall be able to change catalog entries	70	40	40	80	80	
Total Fulfillment	**100**	**55**	**55**	**100**	**100**	**410**
Total Project	**400**	**160**	**160**	**320**	**320**	**1360**

Figure 6-4 Estimates per Subsystem

complete the task in one year (4,160 hours divided by 2,080 hours per year) or it could be accomplished in six months with four people.

Of course, as we all know, in many cases, one cannot just add more people to a project to complete it earlier because of conflicting dependencies and other factors. But, the point is that once the hours are allocated to an organizational element, then resources can be applied against those hours to determine the associated schedule for the organizational element developing the subsystem or Configuration Item. This is just an extension of what we did in Chapter 5, "Determining the Budget."

The point is that the duration of development time for a subsystem or Configuration Item is based on the number of hours estimated for that element divided by the number of resources assigned to the element. However, when assigning resources to a subsystem or Configuration Item, the resulting duration for that element must support the end date of the final project. We discuss how to do this in much more detail in Chapter 7, "Scheduling."

A Final Note

In this chapter, we took a detailed look at how to define a system. However, it is important to realize that systems do not physically exist, nor do subsystems, or for that matter, CIs. These entities are logical groupings of lower pieces. A system is nothing more than a group of subsystems, and a subsystem is just a group of Configuration Items. The only things that actually, physically exist are the components and objects constituting the Configuration Items. This is because components or objects are code. They take up memory and run when a button is clicked on a web page or a program is executed. Components and objects perform the functions the users want the system to accomplish. Everything else is just a logical grouping with no physical reality.

Even so, the concepts of a system, subsystem, and Configuration Item are very important to software designers and managers because they simplify large and complex development efforts. Applying the concepts of a system, subsystem, and Configuration

Item makes planning, managing, and building a complex software system significantly more straightforward.

Now that we understand how to create an effective organization and how to allocate budget to the organizational elements responsible for building the system, the next step is to learn how to create a schedule that will tie it all together. We look at that subject next.

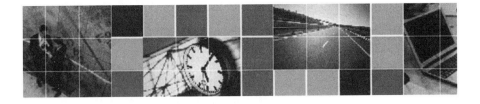

CHAPTER 7

Scheduling

In the previous chapter, we showed how to define a system based on the system requirements and then how to determine an optimum organization to build that system. Once an organization was determined, we learned how to allocate a budget to the elements of the organization responsible for implementing the system requirements.

Allocating pure hours or dollars to organizational elements as was done earlier is only part of the Detailed Planning process. The second part is to turn the hours into a schedule so that the project can be managed. We will tackle that subject next by showing how to create world-class schedules.

Projects always include a schedule. Schedules can be simple, including a few tasks such as analysis, coding, and testing, or complex, containing hundreds of tasks with complicated dependencies. Regardless of how complicated the schedule is, developing a good one is a skill that takes practice. Having an understanding of some basic techniques makes the job a lot easier. In this chapter, we look at the intricacies of developing a world-class schedule and give you everything you need to know in order to schedule any size project from the smallest to the largest. Once you have mastered these skills, you will be well on your way to tracking progress and managing the development effort.

Before we get too far into the details, be forewarned that a schedule is a tool, and as such, serves a purpose. Even so, never rely entirely on a schedule for a complete picture of the project's status. For example, the schedule might show a task significantly behind schedule. However, if you walk over and talk to the developer in charge of that task, he may tell you that he had some trouble with a software driver, but a new driver was just released. The new driver fixes his problems, and he expects to have everything up and running by noon. This is the type of information you will never get from even the best designed schedule.

Types of Schedules

Generally speaking, there are two types of schedules used today. The first is called a Pert chart, which shows dependencies between tasks. The second is the Gantt chart, which is the standard waterfall schedule most often seen on development efforts. In this chapter, we will focus our attention on the Gantt chart, since it is the most common and provides all the information required to manage a development effort.

Levels of Schedules

On a complicated development effort, the key to developing a world-class schedule that is easy to understand and also useable, is to use a hierarchical approach. This means that schedules should be broken down into hierarchical pieces that can be analyzed independently of each other.

This approach serves two purposes. First, executives do not need or want to see low-level details. They want to see the major milestones and the progress toward reaching those milestones. Similarly, developers need much lower-level detail to plan out and execute their efforts. Combining high-level with low-level detail can be difficult if you do not use a hierarchical schedule where each level in the hierarchy provides more detail than the level above. This approach is based on the three-step process listed below:

❑ **Step 1** — Develop the Master Program Schedule

❑ **Step 2** — Develop the Intermediate Program Schedule

❑ **Step 3** — Develop the Lower Level Program Schedule

By taking the three-tiered approach to schedule building, you will be able to develop complicated schedules much more quickly and with fewer errors. Additionally, you will be able to provide scheduling information to many different levels of management, while at the same time, providing each group with only the details they need. We will take a look at each type of schedule and some examples.

Step 1 — Develop the Master Program Schedule

The Master Program Schedule is a high-level schedule that shows the system-level tasks most often of interest to Program Managers and senior executives. These system-level tasks include the start and stop dates for items such as:

❑ Major design reviews

❑ Subsystem analysis

❑ Subsystem design

❑ Subsystem testing

❑ Configuration Item analysis (when there are no subsystems)

❑ Configuration Item design (when there are no subsystems)

❑ Configuration Item testing (when there are no subsystems)

❑ System testing

Master Program Schedules contain all of the scheduling information at the system level. This is the big picture. Details, such as when a Configuration Item's objects are scheduled for coding, are not contained in the Master Program Schedule. This is because the Master Program Schedule should be simple to understand and, if a large number of lower-level tasks are included, it would quickly become too complicated.

Figure 7-1 shows an example of a Master Program Schedule for a hypothetical project. In this example, we will limit ourselves to a few tasks to keep the example understandable. Actual project schedules are much more involved than this. For our purposes, the following schedule will demonstrate the principles we wish to cover.

Task Name	May	June	July	August	Sept.	Oct.	Nov.
System Analysis and Design	▬▬▬▬						
Hardware	▬▬▬						
Configuration Item Analysis			▬▬▬▬				
Configuration Item Design				▬▬▬▬			
CI Coding					▬▬▬▬		
CI Development Testing						▬▬▬	
Acceptance Testing							▬▬▬▬

Figure 7-1 A Master Program Schedule

As Figure 7-1 indicates, the Master Program Schedule shows only key activities with no lower-level detail. Some of the high-level tasks included are Configuration Item analysis and design (in this example, the project was small enough that subsystems were not used) and hardware procurement, but notice that the schedule does not include details required to complete these tasks. For instance, there are no details pertaining to the hardware procurement task, such as getting quotes or generating the purchase order. All that the Master Program Schedule shows is when the activity starts and its duration. Lower-level details are left for the Intermediate Program Schedule and the Lower-Level Schedule.

The Master Program Schedule has two major functions. First, and most importantly, it provides a framework for all Lower-Level schedules. By having the top-level system tasks shown, it is much easier to see where and when the lower-level tasks have to be scheduled since all the lower-level tasks have to be within the start and stop dates shown on the Master Program Schedule.

As an added advantage, using a Master Program Schedule makes working with multiple teams easier because each team can schedule its own activities while still staying in sync with other teams. This is possible because each team uses the same Master Program Schedule milestones, so by definition each team has to stay in sync.

The second use of the Master Program Schedule is for executive reviews. Since the Master Program Schedule contains all the major milestones for the project, but is not cluttered with lower-level detail, it is perfect to use when discussing the project's status with upper management or customers. The bottom line is that no project manager should go anywhere without his or her Master Program Schedule.

Step 2 — Develop the Intermediate Program Schedule

The next level of scheduling detail is contained in the Intermediate Program Schedule. The Intermediate Program Schedule is one level lower than the Master Program Schedule. The Intermediate Program Schedule incorporates the Master Program Schedule's milestones, but breaks those milestones down into lower levels of detail.

Typically, the Intermediate Program Schedule shows the major milestones and tasks associated with each subsystem or Configuration Item. This is an important concept because systems are composed of subsystems and/or Configuration Items.

As established earlier, Configuration Items are self-contained collections of objects and components implementing a related group of functions such as accounting. Taking this concept into consideration, you will see that it makes perfect sense that the Intermediate Program Schedule is often a schedule defining the tasks required to complete Configuration Items.

Like the Master Program Schedule, the Intermediate Program Schedule does not show all the lower-level dates for building the objects and components associated with the Configuration Items, but only the durations of these tasks.

Again, there are several reasons for this, with simplicity being the foremost. There are many low-level details required to complete a Configuration Item, and showing all of them on the Intermediate Program Schedule would make it too complicated. The low-level detail is shown in the Low-Level Schedule.

Based on our Master Program Schedule, we can envision what the Intermediate Program Schedule looks like. As expected, all major tasks contained in the Master Program Schedule are broken out into lower-level tasks, yet all of these tasks sum up to the start and stop dates specified on the Master Program Schedule. The end result is that the Intermediate Program Schedule is a schedule with more detail, but also one that can be more difficult to read.

Figure 7-2 shows the Master Program Schedule expanded to include the Intermediate Program Schedule tasks. For example, the System Analysis and Design Task shown on the Master Program Schedule has been expanded to include:

❑ System requirements

❑ System requirements review

❑ System design

❑ System design review

Similarly, the Configuration Item Analysis and Design tasks shown on the Master Program Schedule have been broken down to show the analysis and design phase durations for the two Configuration Items on the project. As mentioned above, this approach guarantees that the lower-level tasks are scheduled in a time frame that supports the overall system development time frame.

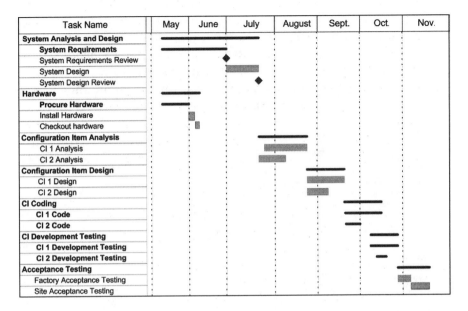

Figure 7-2 An Intermediate Program Schedule

Note that the schedules used here were developed with Microsoft Project. With Microsoft Project, the Intermediate Program Schedule shown in Figure 7-2 can be collapsed into the Master Program Schedule shown in Figure 7-1. This is a feature of the tool that permits users to implement the concepts discussed so far in this chapter.

Step 3 — Develop the Lower-Level Schedule

The final step in developing a project schedule is to develop the Lower-Level Schedule. The principles are exactly the same as those used to develop the Intermediate Program Schedule. However, instead of decomposing the Master Program Schedule tasks, you decompose the Intermediate Program Schedule tasks into low-level tasks.

Figure 7-3 shows our completed schedule, including all the details associated with the Master Program Schedule, the Intermediate Program Schedule, and the Lower-Level Schedule.

Again, Microsoft Project was used to create this schedule. By using this tool we can collapse one level of tasks and end up showing the equivalent of the Intermediate Program Schedule. If we hide another level, we end up showing the equivalent of the Master Program Schedule. Remember that this is just an implementation of the concepts discussed so far.

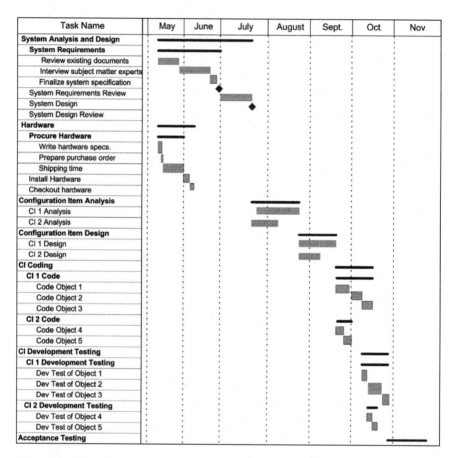

Figure 7-3 A Low-Level Schedule

To keep Figure 7-3 simple, we have not included all of the details typically shown on the Lower-Level schedule. If this schedule were associated with an actual project, these details would be included and the Lower-Level schedule could easily contain several hundred tasks. Once the schedule has been completed, the project manager can turn his attention toward maintaining it. This includes determining the percentage complete for each task on some predefined basis and updating the schedules accordingly. We will take up this subject in the next section.

Determining Schedule Status

Interestingly, many managers do not have a firm handle on how far along they are on a project. They cannot say with confidence whether the project will be completed in a month or six months because they do not have the means to predict how long the remaining effort will take. Needless to say, senior managers and executives do not like this type of uncertainty, as it complicates all aspects of running a business, such as forward budgeting and resource allocation in future quarters. Senior managers are business people who want to be able to plan ahead. They want to know when a new system is going to go online so that they can predict revenues and expenses more accurately.

To provide them with this information, it is important that an accurate schedule status be taken on a regular basis, either weekly or bi-weekly. Regardless of the interval chosen, there are several techniques used to provide a schedule status. They are:

❏ Average milestone

❏ Weighted milestone

❏ 0%–100% complete

❏ Percent start, percent complete

❏ Level of effort

Each technique is discussed below.

Average Milestone

In this method, each task on the schedule is comprised of discreet milestones, and each milestone is given an equal value. For example, if a task consists of four milestones, then each would be given a value of 25 percent. When one of the milestones is finished, the task is 25 percent complete. If two are done, the task is 50 percent complete and so on. Notice that the task cannot be finished until the last milestone is reached, regardless of how much time goes by.

The Average Milestone approach's advantage over other methods is simplicity. Also, keep in mind that the average milestone method becomes more accurate as the number of milestones per task increases.

However, a serious disadvantage of this method is that it assumes each milestone is equally difficult or time consuming to complete. This is often not the case, which is why the weighted milestone approach is sometimes used.

Weighted Milestone

Related to the Average Milestone method is the Weighted Milestone method. Using this method requires that each milestone be given a unique value. For instance, consider the example above. Using the weighted milestone method would mean determining the relative difficulty of each milestone, not an average and equal value, as was the case with the Average Milestone method. Of the four milestones, it might be determined that the first one is easy and is worth 10 percent of the total budget estimated for the task, the next is more difficult and is worth 40 percent, and finally, the last two are worth 25 percent each. Obviously, the percentages for all the milestones constituting a task must equal 100 percent.

This method is more complicated to set up than the average milestone method, but in many cases provides much better visibility into the true schedule status of a task and, ultimately, the project.

0%–100% Complete

The 0%–100% Complete method means that a task cannot have a partially completed status. It is either done or not done at all. This method is not commonly used, but there are instances where it comes in handy.

Consider the case where a server (a Hardware Configuration Item) is on order. It is anticipated that it will take two weeks from the time the server is ordered to the time it is delivered. On the schedule, a task is shown for "Server Delivery" that is two weeks long.

When taking the status of this task, you should note that it does not make sense to say at the end of the first week that the task is 50 percent complete. What would that mean? Does it mean that the server is 50 percent of the way across the country, or that the server is 50 percent built, or something else?

Obviously, it does not mean either, so a better answer would be to say that nothing is done on the task until the server is delivered. Then claim 100 percent completion for the task.

Percent Start, Percent Complete

Related to the 0%–100% Complete method is the Percent Start, Percent Complete method. Using this method, some percentage toward completing the task is claimed when the task is started and the rest is claimed when the task is completely finished.

Like the 0%–100% Complete method, this technique is not often used, but for some circumstances proves useful. Consider the example of the server mentioned above. There may be paperwork to be completed before the server order is sent. In this example, there would still be a task on the schedule called "Order Server," but now this task not only includes shipping, but also some upfront procurement effort. Using the Percent Start, Percent Complete method, when the server is ordered, 20 percent of the task might be considered complete since some procurement activity has been completed. The remaining 80 percent needed for task completion will be realized when the server is delivered.

Level of Effort

Level of effort is generally used for tasks that have no predefined milestones associated with them. A good example is Project Management.

A schedule might show a task running the duration of the project entitled Project Management. There are typically no milestones associated with this task. Instead, the task is completed on a day-by-day basis as the project manager manages the project.

To status this task, one would simply calculate what percentage of the task's total duration has passed and use that as the percentage complete. For example, if the task requires two months to complete, and one month has passed, the task would be 50 percent complete.

Be aware that this is not a very accurate way of determining schedule status in situations when tasks really do consist of milestones, but in some cases it is the only way. However, if a task includes discrete milestones, then Level of Effort should not be used.

Other tasks that might use a Level of Effort approach include: Configuration Management, Quality Assurance, Procurement, and other management functions, such as contractor management.

Understanding Variances

Variances represent values above or below an expected value. With regard to schedules, there can be positive and negative variances, the latter being a situation where the project is behind schedule. A positive schedule variance, on the other hand, indicates that the project is ahead of schedule.

Once the status of a project is known, the next step is to determine the cause of any variances, either positive or negative. Obviously, if the project is ahead of schedule, the percentage complete will be larger than expected — a positive variance. If the project is behind schedule, it will be lower than expected — a negative variance.

In any event, understanding the cause of the variance is as important as knowing that the variance exists.

When completing a variance analysis, there are several things to include. The first, and most obvious, is to specify the cause of the variance accurately. The more accurate you are in this assessment, the easier it will be to take corrective action.

Possible causes of negative variances often revolve around staffing issues, as well as not getting started on a particular part of the project when expected. Other causes include delays in hardware shipments, underestimating the difficulty or volume of work, and loss of key personnel.

The second thing to include in a variance analysis is a corrective action. If the program is running behind schedule, senior management will want to know what steps are being taken to get the project back on track.

On some development efforts, schedule is king and budgets are secondary. In some situations, adding more people to a project can jump-start it again. Another approach is to put the team on overtime. Either approach adds more total hours, which means more work gets done in a given time period.

If adding more people or working overtime are options, they can cause another type of variance called a budget variance. The task or project might be done on time (i.e., without schedule variance), but adding more resources or working longer hours generally causes problems with the budget. We will learn more about budget variances and how to deal with them in the next chapter.

If adding more personnel is not an option, either because the budget is cast in concrete or because personnel with the required skills are not available, the only alternative is to de-scope the project.

In this conversation, scope is used to delineate all the effort agreed to by the stakeholders. Scope is the entire effort that must be expended to complete the project. "De-scoping" means removing some of the work by eliminating some of the requirements. Obviously, if management decides not to build part of the project, there is a better chance that the project can be completed on schedule.

De-scoping is particularly effective when parts of the project can be delayed to a later phase or even permanently deleted. Taking this approach frees up key resources to work on the most critical aspects of the project and is the only way to get a project back on schedule when the budget is anchored.

Finally, variance analysis should discuss impacts to the project caused by the variance. For positive variances, that is, when the project is further along than originally planned, you should still do a variance analysis. This will help identify things that are being done correctly, leading to overall schedule improvements.

A Caveat

The limitation of any schedule status is that it does not necessarily do well at predicting a project's end date. Therefore, when making an estimate to completion, be sure to factor in the difficulty of the remaining effort as it pertains to the original estimate. Similarly, do not forget to factor in the positive side of having completed difficult portions of the project. In this case, the project might actually be finished sooner than expected.

With that said, the completeness metric, when used with other techniques such as critical path analysis, will give you a very good tool to manage the effort. For instance, if it is discovered after getting well into the design phase that there is still a great deal of requirements analysis that has not been completed, it is time to take corrective action. For any project manager, this type of information can spell the difference between disaster and success on a project.

The Relationship Between the Project Estimate and the Project Schedule

In Chapter 5, "Determining the Budget," we showed how to use the hours estimated for a task to determine the duration of the task. For example, if a design task was estimated at 480 hours to complete, and three people are assigned to the task, then the duration of that task would be one month (assuming 160 hours in a month).

The fact that we can calculate a task duration based on the number of hours estimated for that task divided by the number of people working on the task gives us the beginning of our schedule.

However, knowing that the duration for a task is one month does not show the relationship between a task and other tasks on the project. This is what the schedule does. We can get duration from the estimate, but we have to put the task on a schedule to show when it starts and ends and how it relates to all the other tasks on the project. For example, schedules show us the critical path, or which task must be completed before the next one starts. We do not see this relationship from the durations calculated from the original estimate.

A problem that often arises when comparing a task duration derived from the original estimate and the duration for the task shown on the schedule is that the two may not match up exactly. For example, a task might be estimated at 32 hours and one person. In other words, the task will take 80 percent of a week to complete. However, on the schedule the task might be shown as being one week long. A reason for the discrepancy might be that a resource will, as a practical matter, be involved with the task all week, not just Monday through Thursday.

Similarly, a task might be estimated at 42 hours but be shown on the schedule as taking an even week to complete. For example, the resource assigned to the task might have another assignment starting the following week, and so from a practical standpoint, the task is shortened by two hours to accommodate a real-world limitation. These types of discrepancies and rounding errors are natural as they reflect the reality of actually managing key personnel versus the pure view of a project created through the estimate.

Typically, the overall estimate should not be significantly different from the hours derived by looking at the duration of tasks on the schedule because some tasks might be shortened while others are lengthened to account for resource availability and other practical matters. The pluses tend to cancel out the minuses with the end result that calculating hours based on task duration from the schedule is not materially different from the hours calculated in the original estimate.

The one thing to be careful about is to ensure that the process of creating the schedule does not materially change the total hours estimated for an individual task to such a degree that it is no longer valid.

As a practical matter, keep in mind that not every task shown on the schedule has an associated time-phased budget. For example, on most software development schedules there will be a major task called coding. On the schedule, this task most likely will consist of sub-tasks pertaining to coding particular objects and components for which there is no associated time-phased budget.

The coding task should have been estimated based on the system requirements and the estimate turned into a component of the time-phased budget. As the project progresses and enters the coding phase and more details are known about the objects and components that have to be coded, the coding sub-tasks are often added to the schedule. This is fine as long as the sub-task durations do not exceed the primary task's duration.

Now that we know how to create the project's budget and schedule, the next step is to learn how to manage both using a Cost and Schedule Control System. We will turn our attention to that next.

PART 2

Managing
the Project

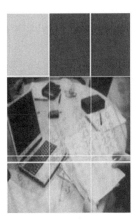

PART 2 OF THIS BOOK focuses on managing a software project. In the following chapters you will learn how to:

❏ Set up a Cost and Schedule Control System

❏ Use the Cost and Schedule Control System to manage the project's cost

❏ Use the Cost and Schedule Control System to manage the project's schedule

❏ Manage changes

❏ Manage quality

Part 2 of this book contains everything you need to complete your projects on time and on budget.

CHAPTER 8

Managing Cost and Schedule

Up to this point we have learned how to create the estimate for a project, to turn that estimate into a budget, to allocate the budget to the organizational elements responsible for doing the work, and, finally, how to create a schedule capturing when tasks start and end and the relationship between the tasks. When all of this is complete, the Detailed Planning phase is over and the project starts. Once started, it is the project manager's job to manage the project according to the original cost and schedule estimates. With that goal in mind, we now turn our attention from planning activities to learning how to manage the project according to the original schedule and budget.

One of the hardest parts of building software is determining how well the project is going. This means knowing not only the schedule status, but also the budget status. In this chapter, you will learn how to use a sophisticated management tool called the Cost and Schedule Control System (CSCS) that allows a project manager to determine not only schedule status, but also budget status.

Three Elements of a CSCS

Before getting into the details of actually setting up and running a cost and schedule control system, we need to cover a few definitions. A software project has three cost and schedule factors associated with it. These are:

1. Budget — the agreed to dollar amount needed to complete the project. This is what the project owner agreed to pay for the entire effort. This is not the actual money or cash paid to complete the effort but rather the plan for expenditures. The budget includes all elements of the project, and, when defining a budget, it is important to include items such as:

❏ Development

❏ Testing

❏ Hardware

❏ Travel

❏ Training

❏ Marketing

The above items are called cost elements and are typically defined in a Statement of Work and estimated. Of course, your project will have other cost elements. It is important to identify all elements of cost before the actual budget is determined so that the entire budget for the project can be accurately estimated.

We will use the acronym BCWS, which stands for Budgeted Cost of Work Scheduled, to mean the budget.

One very important rule about budgets (i.e., BCWS) is that they are cast in stone once the project starts. If the project is overrunning the budget, the budget is not changed. Rather, the overrun is shown as a variance against the original budget. In other words, if the budget for a project is $1 million, and half way through the project, estimates to complete the project indicate that the entire effort is going to cost $1.5 million, the budget is still $1 million, but there is now a $500,000 variance to the original $1 million budget.

The reason for this rule is fairly straightforward. If budgets were changed, there would be no way to tell how much the project is overrunning or under-running against the original plan. Therefore, budgets are not changed when the project gets into trouble or for that matter when it is coming in early. When we discuss the actual costs of the project below, you will see how to handle overruns or under-runs.

Like all rules, there are always exceptions. The one exception is this: if the scope of the project changes, the budget changes. In other words, if there is new functionality added to the project after the project starts, then the budget has to be changed to reflect this new work. Added or deleted scope is the only reason the budget is changed.

Remember, even though budgets do not change, that fact does not preclude the team from overrunning or under-running the budget. What is actually spent — called "actuals" — is discussed below.

2. **Actual Costs** — These are the costs that show up on timesheets and invoices. Actual costs are the costs incurred from doing the work. Obviously, actual cost increases as the program continues. On a very well run program, actual cost should equal the budget, which represents the planned expenditures. Actual costs include items such as hardware purchases, labor hours billed, and travel expenses. We will use the acronym ACWP for Actual Cost of Work Performed to indicate actual costs incurred on the project.

3. **Budgeted Cost of Work Performed** — The Budgeted Cost of Work Performed or BCWP is the value of the effort performed to date. This is the value assigned to a major milestone on the devel-

opment schedule. For instance, if the plan required 100 hours to write a requirements specification, and the effort is finished, then the BCWP for that milestone is 100 hours times the hourly rate of those who worked on the specification. If the requirements specification is half completed, then the BCWP is 50 hours times the hourly rate of those working on the effort.

Do not confuse budgets (BCWS), Actual Cost of Work Performed (ACWP), and Budgeted Cost of Work Performed (BCWP). They are three distinct items. Budgets never change unless the scope of the project changes. Both BCWP and ACWP increase during the project and can be either equal in value or differ from the budget (i.e., BCWS).

Importance of the Three Elements of CSCS

So why do we need three pieces of data to manage the project? The answer is simple. Taken together, the three items indicate whether the project is on schedule and also whether the project is overrunning, under-running, or on budget.

All three elements are required because, at any given time, the project could be:

❑ Overrunning but ahead of schedule

❑ Overrunning but behind schedule

❑ Overrunning but on schedule

❑ Under-running but behind schedule

❑ Under-running but ahead of schedule

❑ Under-running but on schedule

Here is how it works.

How to Use BCWP, ACWP, and BCWS

To set up a cost and schedule control system for your project, there are five steps to follow:

❏ **Step 1** — Establish the budget

❏ **Step 2** — Define the completion criteria

❏ **Step 3** — Establish a schedule

❏ **Step 4** — Graph the BCWS curve

❏ **Step 5** — Manage the effort

Each step is explained in the following sections.

Step 1 — Establish the Budget

The first step in setting up a cost and schedule control system is to establish the budget. Remember that the budget is the amount it will cost to finish the project. Remember also that the budget must include all elements of cost such as development tasks, travel, and hardware procurement. We will leave everything but development costs out of this example to keep it simple, but for most projects, there are many other costs that must be budgeted.

Let us take a look at an example to see the details (this is the same example used in Chapter 5, "Determining the Budget," but the details are shown here once again for convenience).

Assume that the team has been given the task of building an enterprise-wide website project. The Statement of Work indicates that the following tasks have to be completed:

❏ Write a requirements specification (i.e., complete analysis)

❏ Develop a top-level design

❏ Develop a detailed design

❏ Code the software

❏ Test the final product

Executives want to know how much all of this is going to cost, so the project manager, after collecting and analyzing the system requirements, provides them with the following estimate:

❏   Write a requirements specification — 400 hours

❏   Develop a top-level design — 160 hours

❏   Develop a detailed design — 160 hours

❏   Code the software — 320 hours

❏   Test the final product — 320 hours

Based on these estimates, the total budget for the project is 1,360 hours. This number is known as the Budget At Completion or BAC.

Step 2 — Define the Completion Criteria

The next step, defining the completion criteria, is very important. The completion criteria for a task is a well-defined point that, when met, indicates the task is complete. Without getting into the details, suffice it to say that sometimes completion criteria are easy to specify and other times difficult. A good example of the latter is the requirements specification, for which it can be difficult to specify what constitutes completion, versus something more straightforward such as test criteria. You will have to exercise judgment on determining completion criteria for each project task, using experience as a guide.

To return to our example, suppose we defined the following completion criteria for each task as shown in Figure 8-1 below:

Item	Size	Hours	Total	Completion Criteria
Requirements Specification	10 sections	40 hours per section	400 hours	Sign off by executives
Preliminary Design	8 objects	20 hours per object	160 hours	Successful completion of Preliminary Design Review
Detailed Design	8 objects	20 hours per object	160 hours	Successful completion of Detailed Design Review
Code	8 objects	40 hours per object	320 hours	Successful completion of Development Testing
Test	8 objects	40 hours per object	320 hours	Completion of Factory Acceptance Testing

Figure 8-1 Defining the Completion Criteria

The completion criteria are used to determine Budgeted Cost of Work Performed, or BCWP.

Relationship Between Completion Criteria and the Schedule
In Chapter 7, "Scheduling," we discussed how to determine schedule status. In that chapter we learned that there are several techniques to status a schedule. These include:

❏   Average milestone method

❏   Weighted milestone method

❏   0%–100% complete method

❑ Percent start, percent complete method

❑ Level of effort method

The relationship between the completions criteria described in Step 2 and the techniques used to status a schedule is that they are one and the same. In other words, once the completion criteria are established, they become the method used to status the schedule.

From Figure 8-1, it is easy to see that the completion criteria are actually the weighted milestone schedule status method (which in this example happens to be the same as if the average milestone method were chosen).

Step 3 — Establish a Schedule

The next step is to assign personnel to the tasks and lay out the schedule. Suppose that during the first part of the project you can assign two and a half people to develop the requirements specification. This task has been estimated at 400 hours. Two and one half people working on it means that it will be completed in one month.

Note that when you lay out resources, you should be sure to use the expected time utilization factor for the project. Theoretically, there are about 2,080 hours in a year, but realistically, because of vacations, holidays, and sick time, no one works that many hours. Furthermore, November and December are notoriously bad months for scheduling due to the holidays. Also keep in mind that senior employees generally have more vacation time than junior employees. That should be factored into the schedule.

Finally, in the example as before, assume 160 hours per month. Of course, some months are longer and some are shorter. If your estimate needs to be very accurate, use an accounting calendar to determine the actual number of working hours in each month.

Moving back to our example, assume there can only be two people working half time on the preliminary design. At that rate, it will take one month to complete.

There is one person working on the detailed design. The rest of the time, there are two full-time people working on the effort. With this information, it is easy to develop the schedule shown in Figure 8-2 below.

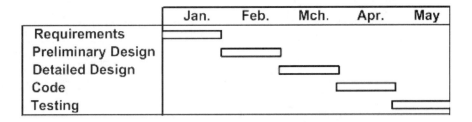

Figure 8-2 Project Schedule

By taking this approach, the schedule is directly related to the budget. Unfortunately, on many projects, this is not the case. *Remember, the only way to manage a software development effort is to correlate budget with schedule.*

Step 4 — Graph Budgeted Cost of a Work-Scheduled (BCWS) Curve

Once the budget and schedule have been determined, the next step is to determine the time-phased budget. This is simply the budget laid out over some periodic time scale such as months or quarters. In this example, we will use months.

Remember, the resources working on the project cost $50 per hour. Based on this rate, the total cost for each task can be calculated, and these costs are shown in Figure 8-3 below. Using this information with the expected task duration gives us the following budget, which combined with the schedule, gives us the time-phased budget.

Task	Duration (Hours)	Rate ($ Per hour)	Budget
Requirements	400	$50	$20,000
Preliminary Design	160	$50	$8,000
Detailed Design	160	$50	$8,000
Code	320	$50	$16,000
Testing	320	$50	$16,000
Total	1360		$68,000

Figure 8-3 Total Cost For Each Task

By combining this information with the schedule, you can determine the time-phased budget as shown in Figure 8-4.

	January	February	March	April	May
Requirements	$20,000				
Preliminary Design		$8,000			
Detailed Design			$8,000		
Code				$16,000	
Testing					$16,000
Total	$20,000	$8,000	$8,000	$16,000	$16,000

Figure 8-4 Total Cost For Each Task

Completing the steps above provides the project manager with some very important management tools. The project manager knows what the schedule is, what the budget per month is, and what resources are required to satisfy not only the schedule, but also the monthly budget.

Using that information, we can generate a BCWS curve shown in Figure 8-5 below.

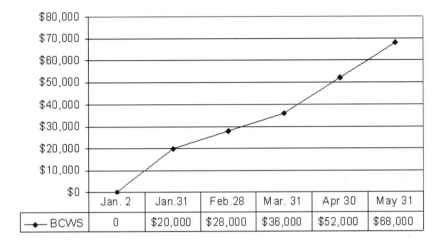

	Jan. 2	Jan.31	Feb.28	Mar. 31	Apr 30	May 31
BCWS	0	$20,000	$28,000	$36,000	$52,000	$68,000

Figure 8-5 BCWS Curve

Take a look at the first month. The budget goes from zero when the project starts to $20,000 at the end of the month. This is because the schedule says the requirements specification will be completed in the first month. We know that this effort is worth $20,000 because it was estimated to take 400 hours to complete at $50.00 per hour.

The budget curve (a graph of BCWS) is just a running total, which is the sum of the time-phased budget value for each month. February starts at $20,000 and adds the preliminary design effort to finish the month at $28,000 ($20,000 + top-level design effort, which is equal to 160 hours times $50.00 per hour).

The process is continued for the rest of the effort with each month adding the amount for that month (from the time-phased budget) to the running total. This is how the budget curve is determined.

It is very important to remember that the budget curve never changes unless the scope of the effort is changed (new tasks are added to the effort or old tasks are removed from the effort). Once the budget has been created, it never changes even though the effort might be overrunning or under-running. This is discussed in more detail in the following sections.

Step 5 — Manage the Effort

What has been accomplished so far does not get us to the ultimate goal of being able to manage the effort. To do so requires that we consider some more data in addition to the time-phased budget, namely the value of the work completed, and the cost of performing that work.

Remember, the value of the work accomplished is called the Budgeted Cost of Work Performed (BCWP), and the actual cost of doing the work is called the Actual Cost of Work Performed (ACWP).

Both BCWP and ACWP are different from the Budgeted Cost of Work Scheduled determined by the time-phased budget.

Combining all of these facts together makes it possible to track the progress of the project accurately. In the subsequent paragraphs, we will follow the project through completion using all the concepts above.

Suppose This Happens In January
Suppose that at the end of January the team tells the project manager that eight sections of the Software Requirements Specification are complete. The Project manager tells executive management that $16,000 of effort is done and that this effort cost $22,000. The project manager claims that the project is *on schedule* and *on budget*.

Is the project manager correct? Is the project on schedule and actually on budget? Let us see. Take a look at Figure 8-6 below.

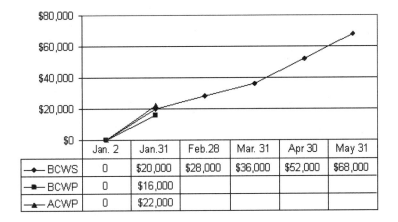

Figure 8-6 Project Is Over Budget And Behind Schedule

Based on the graph, the answer is *no*. The truth is that the project is behind schedule and overrunning the budget.

Why? Because the schedule says that the team should have finished the entire requirements specification. In reality, only eight sections have been completed. We can calculate how far off the plan we are with the following equation:

BCWP - BCWS = $16,000 - $20,000 = -$4,000

(The $16,000 comes from eight sections of the requirements specification times 40 hours per section times $50.00 per hour.)

This calculation tells us that we are a negative $4,000 off the plan. By this we mean that we had planned on doing $20,000 worth of work in January, but in reality only got $16,000 of it done. So the project is behind schedule. This is called a *schedule variance*.

What about the second part of the question, namely is the project on budget as the project manager claims? The graph above tells us that the answer is "no," the budget has been overrun since the project manager claims that $22,000 was spent so far.

Where did the $22,000 come from? When the project manager realized that the project was behind schedule, he asked the team to work overtime in order to catch up. Instead of spending 400 hours on the project, as was budgeted, and spending $20,000 (400 hours x $50/ hour = $20,000), the team actually spent 440 hours and $22,000 on the effort as shown below:

440 hours x $50/ hour = $22,000.

If the requirement specification had been completed, the team could have earned a maximum of $20,000 in BCWP. However, the project manager confused the ACWP, which is equal to $22,000, with BCWS, which is $20,000. Taken together, the three measurements, namely BCWS, BCWP, and ACWP, show that the *cost variance* equals the BCWP minus ACWP ($16,000 - $22,000 = -$6,000).

Suppose This Happens in February
In February the team finishes up the requirements specification. Executive management takes a hard line and tells the team that they are behind schedule. Take a look at the new set of curves shown in Figure 8-7 below:

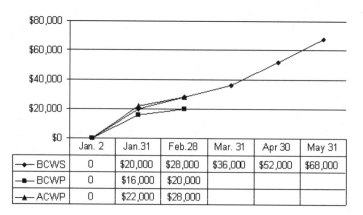

	Jan. 2	Jan.31	Feb.28	Mar. 31	Apr 30	May 31
BCWS	0	$20,000	$28,000	$36,000	$52,000	$68,000
BCWP	0	$16,000	$20,000			
ACWP	0	$22,000	$28,000			

Figure 8-7 Project Is On Budget And Behind Schedule

Is senior management correct? Is the team behind schedule? The answer is *yes*.

The project is behind schedule because the top-level design was supposed to have been completed in February. However, only the requirements specification was completed. The BCWP is $20,000 because this was the BCWP for the requirements specification. The project is on budget because ACWP is now equal to BCWS, but that is a different fact from the fact that the project is behind schedule.

In March, the Following Happens

❏ The team finishes up the preliminary design

❏ The team finishes up the detailed design

❏ The team claims another $16,000 in BCWP

The graph below shows the updated situation. Notice that BCWP equals the BCWS. The project is no longer behind schedule as shown in Figure 8-8 below:

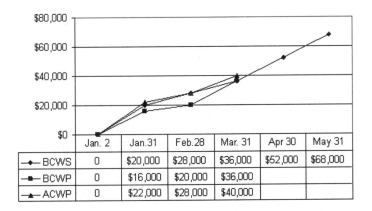

	Jan. 2	Jan.31	Feb.28	Mar. 31	Apr 30	May 31
—◆— BCWS	0	$20,000	$28,000	$36,000	$52,000	$68,000
—■— BCWP	0	$16,000	$20,000	$36,000		
—▲— ACWP	0	$22,000	$28,000	$40,000		

Figure 8-8 Project is Over Budget And On Schedule

The project is overrunning because the team worked extra hours to catch up. ACWP is now equal to $40,000 ($22,000 in January + $6,000 in February + $12,000 in March = $40,000 total).

However, the project is on schedule because the team finished up the requirements ($20,000), the top level design ($8,000), and the detailed design ($8,000). Adding up the numbers gives a BCWP equal to $36,000, which is equal to the budget (i.e., BCWS) through the end of March.

Suppose the following happens in April

❑ The team finishes up the coding

❑ The project manager accrues $12,000 in ACWP

What is the situation now? The answer is, the project is on schedule and no longer overrunning.

This is the case because BCWS = BCWP = ACWP = $52,000. Figure 8-9 shows the details.

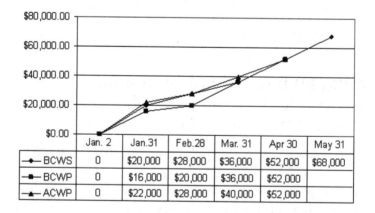

	Jan. 2	Jan.31	Feb.28	Mar. 31	Apr 30	May 31
BCWS	0	$20,000	$28,000	$36,000	$52,000	$68,000
BCWP	0	$16,000	$20,000	$36,000	$52,000	
ACWP	0	$22,000	$28,000	$40,000	$52,000	

Figure 8-9 Project Is On Schedule And On Budget

If everything goes according to plan from this point forward, the team will be very successful at finishing the project on time and on schedule. Let us see what happens.

Finally in May
The team:

❑   Finishes up testing of the new project

❑   Takes credit for the final $16K in ACWP

Figure 8-10 indicates the final curves showing that the project was finished on schedule and on budget.

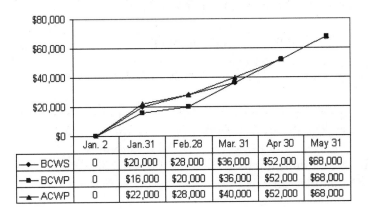

	Jan. 2	Jan.31	Feb.28	Mar. 31	Apr 30	May 31
BCWS	0	$20,000	$28,000	$36,000	$52,000	$68,000
BCWP	0	$16,000	$20,000	$36,000	$52,000	$68,000
ACWP	0	$22,000	$28,000	$40,000	$52,000	$68,000

Figure 8-10 Project Finishes On time And On Budget

Creating an Estimate at Completion

Recall that we defined the Budget at Completion (BAC) as the total budget for the project. If one adds up the total budget (either hours or dollars) for all the tasks, the final number is the BAC. This number represents the end point of the BCWS curve.

As the project progresses, ACWP and BCWP can be either greater or less than BCWS, which at that point in time means that the project may or may not come in on budget.

Sometimes a project can be behind schedule, but the project manager knows that the upcoming work will go very quickly and that the project will get back on schedule. Or, perhaps there was difficulty getting the project started, and the company may never be able to overcome the deficit created in the beginning.

Regardless of the cause, if the project is going to be over or under the BAC at the end of the project, the project manager must account for this. This is accomplished by calculating an Estimate At Completion (EAC). The EAC reflects how much the project is *estimated* to be over or under the BAC. Until the project is finished, this is an estimate that usually changes on a month-to-month basis. That is why it is called an Estimate at Completion.

The easiest way to understand how to create an EAC is to look at a simple example. Assume the BAC for a project is 10,000 hours (we will use hours instead of dollars to make the example easier to understand).

Assume that halfway through the project, the BCWS is 5,000 hours, the BCWP is 4,000 hours and the ACWP is 5,000 hours. In this case, the project is behind schedule by 1,000 hours (i.e., BCWS (5,000) minus BCWP (4,000) equals 1,000 hours of work not completed). The project, however, is on budget.

Even though the project is on budget, there is a problem since there are still 5,000 hours of work remaining, plus 1,000 hours of work that have to be made up. This is where the EAC comes into play.

If everything is linear, and the project manager believes that the remaining work will be completed as planned, and that the 1,000 hours of delinquent work will get done in 1,000 hours, then the EAC would be 11,000 hours. This is based on the fact that from this point forward, the team will do the remaining 5,000 hours of work plus finish the delinquent 1,000 hours of work.

It is not always the case that the EAC is simply the addition of the delta, or change, in BCWP or ACWP to BCWS. Consider again the above example. The project manager might decide that the delinquent 1,000 hours of work (which is based on the original estimate for this work) was actually underestimated. It might be determined that the delinquent 1,000 hours of work is actually very difficult and will require 2,000 hours to complete. In this case the EAC would be 12,000 hours. This is calculated by adding 2,000 hours of work (the delinquent effort) to the original BAC (10,000 hours).

Another possibility is that the project manager might decide that the delinquent effort is actually much easier to complete than originally expected and will only require 500 additional hours (not 1,000 hours) to complete. In this case the EAC would be 10,500 hours.

Regardless of the situation, determining the EAC requires a detailed understanding of both the ACWP and BCWP. These two parameters have to be evaluated carefully. Based on that analysis, an EAC can be determined.

Regardless of the EAC, BAC does not change. BAC represents the original plan against which the estimated outcome is compared. In our example above, if BAC is 10,000 hours and EAC is 11,000 hours, the project manager is forewarning management that the project is going to come in 1,000 hours over the originally planned budget.

EAC should be calculated at regular intervals throughout the project. Typically, it is updated on a monthly basis. A shorter period of time generally has too much "noise" in the reporting of BCWP and ACWP to be accurate. Going longer than a month might mean failing to identify a problem early and thus also failing to notify senior management about it.

The cost and schedule control system described in this chapter is a very effective technique for showing the current status of the development effort and for projecting the status at completion.

Using this technique, you will always know the status of the entire project as well as the individual pieces.

Now that we have a good handle on how to manage a project against the original budget and schedule, we can turn our attention to two other important subjects, managing changes to the project once it starts and managing quality on the project. Both of these subjects are important since they can significantly impact a project's budget and schedule.

CHAPTER 9

Managing Change

Up to this point we have spent a great deal of time detailing how to plan and manage a complicated software development effort. As is always the case, the upfront planning, by necessity, is based on an estimate. Factors that occur during the project often combine to make the preliminary estimates less accurate as the project progresses. Obviously, if the initial estimates are not accurate, the project will not be completed on time and on budget. This situation must be accounted for.

Items impacting the initial estimate include adding forgotten tasks and changing functionality. The process of managing and controlling changes, and ultimately of controlling the cost and schedule baseline, is called Configuration Management. In this chapter, we will discuss how to use a well-designed Configuration Management system to ensure that your project comes in on time and on budget.

An important aspect of any software development effort is the ability to control changes to completed products such as specifications and code. Controlling change is one of the main functions of Configuration Management (CM). If changes are not controlled in an organized manner, then chaos may result. Consider, for example, a requirements specification. If the content of this document is allowed to change in an uncontrolled manner after the key stakeholders agree to its content, then the project will experience numerous and expensive schedule slips.

Every project manager knows about the infamous "requirements creep" problem. Requirements creep means that there is a steady increase in the number of requirements and also changes to existing requirements as the project progresses. Finally, the cost of all these changes becomes significant, with the result that the schedule and budget are in total disarray. This is what CM is all about, controlling those changes, and when they are accepted, having a process that documents the cost and schedule impact.

Another reason to control change is to ensure that everyone involved with the project uses the same version of a product. If, for example, requirements are changed on a regular basis, and those changes are not communicated to the development team, developers may be building products to the wrong specification.

CM encompasses other functions besides just controlling change. These include identification, reporting, and maintaining a library, in addition to change management. Figure 9-1 shows these functions.

Identification is the scheme used to identify the parts of a software system. This scheme generally includes a naming convention for documentation and code as well as a numbering scheme for each product. Part numbers are used in software the same as any other industry. They uniquely identify a specific product like a specification.

CM also includes the important function of librarian. The CM library is a physical or electronic location where all software development products are stored. Libraries can be physical, but more often are electronic. Examples of products stored in the CM library include specifications, code, and test results.

Finally, CM includes a reporting function. This allows everyone on the team to know the status of various products and the identification associated with each.

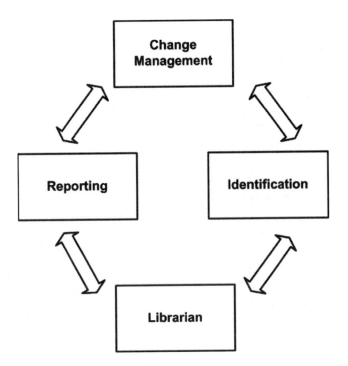

Figure 9-1 Typical CM Functions

Taken together, these functions form the basis from which all software products can be controlled, and more importantly, released. By "released" we mean the general distribution of a product in its final form. Consider code for example. Certainly, before any code is loaded onto the production servers, the development team and management will want to ensure that it is the final version of the software. Once that point has been reached, the code can be released, meaning everyone agrees that it can be loaded onto the production servers and used.

In the following sections we will take a look at each of the above functions and describe in detail how to implement them on your project.

Creating Baselines

The discussion begins with the definition of a baseline. A baseline is a product, such as a design document, which is not only complete but has also been approved by project stakeholders. In other words, key stakeholders have agreed that the product is finished and is correct. This does not mean that at some point in the future a completed product cannot be changed, only that if it is changed, then there is some means of controlling that change.

When we speak of control, we are referring to controlling changes to that product.

This idea is straightforward. There are activities associated with developing any product, such as generating a requirements specification that is part of the development life cycle. In the case of a requirements specification, these activities occur during the system analysis phase, when the requirements for the project are collected and refined. During this process, many changes take place. New requirements are added, and existing requirements are dropped. Requirements are modified and refined until the team feels that they accurately represent what the business unit wants.

You could say that during this initial phase of requirements-gathering activities, the requirements are under *development-level control*. In other words, the team has a responsibility for gathering the requirements and ensuring their accuracy, completeness, and testability. At this time, the team has complete control of changes to the requirements specification.

At some point, the analysis activity must end or the software system will never get built. Work must move forward from analysis to completing a design based on those requirements. After that, coding and testing must be completed.

Note that this discussion used the concepts of requirements and a requirements specification. Of course, if your development methodology generates some other type of product, such as Use Cases, the principles are the same. At some point, every product/artifact or whatever you wish to call it, must be controlled from a change standpoint.

To return to the original discussion: consider what happens if a requirement changes late in the project's life cycle, perhaps even during the testing phase. The impact of this end-game change is more significant than if the change had been made much earlier in the process.

Someone has to own up to this impact. Someone must agree to incur the cost and schedule impacts associated with the change. This is precisely why products, such as the requirements specification, are baselined. With a baseline, the project manager can control a change and, when a change is necessary, the cost and schedule impacts can be determined and agreed to by the stakeholders in the project, especially the ones responsible for the budget and schedule.

A baseline, when it is established, says in effect that all the stakeholders have agreed a product is finished. Finishing a product means that the next phase of the development activity, which depends on those finished products, can be started without risk.

Of course, this does not imply that a change cannot happen late in the game. Changes do occur at all points in the development effort. Everything cannot be foreseen at the start. Some things have to be changed as the project progresses. But, a baseline is a very good way to control those changes.

With the definition of a baseline under our belt, the next question becomes which products should be baselined?

Figure 9-2 lists key products that make good candidates for baselining.

❑ Budgets

❑ Schedules

❑ System Requirements

❑ Software Requirements

❑ Design Documents

❑ Code

❑ Test Plans

❑ Test Procedures

❑ Test Results

Figure 9-2
Product to Baseline

While looking over the products in Figure 9-2, most readers will agree that changes do occur to these products after they have been baselined. As a matter of fact, major changes often occur. It is not unusual to have a system requirement change during testing.

Since change is inevitable, the issue becomes how to control those changes. We will consider that next, as we look at how reviews are used in conjunction with a Configuration Management system.

Conducting Reviews

A review is a meeting of key stakeholders to determine whether a product, such as a design document, is finished and correct. As mentioned above, when a review is done, and the reviewers consider the product correct and finished, that product is considered baselined.

It is easy to identify the most important products generated on a typical development effort. These products include items such as code, specifications, and design documents. The list of products is used to determine the key reviews that should be conducted on a major development effort. Below we take a look at each review and what should be covered.

Reviewing the System Requirements

By completing this review, you will ensure that developers and stakeholders agree to the system-level requirements.

In the methodology described in this book, system requirements are collected during the Detailed Planning phase. Because of their importance to estimating, the system requirements should be reviewed and approved before the cost estimate is completed.

Reviewing the Software Requirements

Software requirements, as used here, are the detailed, low-level requirements, used by developers to design and build the system. By completing the software requirements review, all stakeholders are assured that developers understand exactly what they have to build. You also ensure that the requirements are accurate, complete, and testable.

Software requirements should be reviewed before design begins. Otherwise, if the requirements change, significant aspects of the design might also have to be changed, causing cost and schedule problems.

Keep in mind that not all the software requirements have to be reviewed at the same time. For example, if a system consists of multiple Configuration Items, each Configuration Item can have separate software requirements reviews. Even for a Configuration Item's software requirements, different blocks of software requirements can be reviewed at different times.

The only point about the timing of the software requirements review or reviews is that the software requirements should be reviewed before serious design effort is started.

Reviewing the Design

By completing this review, you ensure that the design is the optimum design required to implement the requirements. You also ensure that every requirement has a design element associated with it and that every design element actually implements a requirement. This last factor eliminates the tendency of developers to build more into the software than is required.

Design reviews should be done before coding is started. Otherwise, changes to the design could necessitate rewriting significant blocks of code. Obviously, this type of situation will most likely impact the project's cost and schedule.

Reviewing the Code

Code review, as used here, is not the same as a code walkthrough or a code inspection. Rather, code review as used here, is a review of the code to determine whether it can be baselined. For example, a code review might be conducted before Acceptance Testing, which is discussed in detail in Chapter 11.

Purpose of a Review

To gain a better understanding of the purpose and scope of a review, consider for example a System Requirements Review.

Attending this review are the stakeholders, developers, and, in some instances, senior management. Upon completing this review, the stakeholders are in effect saying, "Yes, this is what we want you to build."

Similarly, at the completion of the requirements review, the developers are agreeing that they understand what the stakeholders want them to build and that the requirements are technically feasible.

The System Requirements Review forms the contract between developers and stakeholders as to the scope of the development effort and serves to clarify ambiguities that might exist in the requirements.

Other reviews are similar in nature, but, in some instances, the attendance list changes. Use Figure 9-3 as a checklist to determine whom to invite to each type of review.

One point to keep in mind is that the longer a product goes without being baselined, the greater the program risk because no agreement has been reached about the "goodness" of the product being developed.

However, a product that is baselined too early will usually cause a great deal of change traffic, which is equally bad. A balance between risk and the administrative overhead associated with maintaining the baseline are the key factors in determining when a review should occur. Careful consideration should be given to each. As a general rule, never baseline a product before it is truly complete.

Making Changes to Baselined Products

Once a baseline has been established, the next question becomes, "How to control changes to it?" The answer is through change requests.

Change requests are written whenever a baseline needs to be changed.

A change request must include a list of the products affected by the change, such as documentation or code. This is an important point because changes occurring toward the end of a project will likely impact multiple baselines (i.e., products) such as requirements specifications, design documents, and code. Other information contained on the change request includes whether the change has been accepted and the cost and schedule impacts associated with the change.

From a logistics standpoint, change requests are best handled electronically. This can be accomplished by setting up a database containing the required information. This approach not only makes entering and managing data easier, but also will allow searches and queries on any of the fields on your change request.

Further, since change requests are managed through the Engineering and Change Control Boards (discussed next), electronic versions allow for a convenient way to take minutes at these meetings.

System Requirements Review
- Project Manager
- Developers
- Configuration Management
- Quality Assurance
- Stakeholders

Software Requirements Review
- Development Manager
- CI Team Leads
- Configuration Management
- Quality Assurance
- Legacy System Managers
- Other Stakeholders

Design Review
- Development Manager
- CI Team Leads
- Development Team
- Configuration Management
- Quality Assurance
- Other Stakeolders

Code Reviews
- Development Manager
- CI Team Leads
- Development Team
- Configuration Management
- Quality Assurance
- Other Stakeholders

Figure 9-3 Review Participants

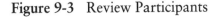

There are commercially available tools designed to handle Configuration Management, including change requests. For a larger project, you might want to consider purchasing one of these tools.

How to Decide Whether to Accept a Proposed Change to a Baselined Product

Deciding whether to accept or reject a proposed change is the responsibility of the change control boards. The concept of change control boards is central to having an effective CM organization. Without these boards, the whole concept of change control would be moot, since there would be no central authority to approve the cost and schedule impacts associated with the change. This is how projects get completely out of control and end up overrunning both budget and schedule.

Of course, for smaller projects, these boards might actually consist of a person or two. This is fine because the idea is to centralize the approval authority for baseline changes. As long as the process described below is followed, the size of the board does not matter.

That said, there is one caveat. The board must be large enough so that all stakeholders have representation on the board. This allows all involved to provide input about the impact of the change. Large projects have many stakeholders. A change that is good for one group might not be good for the others. In the case of large projects, boards are going to consist of more than just a few individuals.

When the board meets, it must make a decision based on two things. First, it should decide whether the change makes sense technically. For example, will the change affect so many other things that there is no reasonable justification for incurring that much technical chaos? Or perhaps a change cannot be implemented technically. Perhaps the change request is asking for a change in performance not achievable with the existing infrastructure or technology.

The second issue is the impact on the project's budget resulting from an approved change. Generally, no change is without some cost. Sometimes the cost is large, other times small. Also, keep in mind that budget changes often impact the schedule as well.

Since determining whether a change is technically feasible is different from determining whether the company can afford it, there are two boards involved in evaluating the change. The first board is called the Engineering Review Board (ERB), and it has the job of determining the technical feasibility of the change. The Engineering Review Board also determines the impact to the project if the change is approved. The impact is specified in both cost and schedule impacts.

The chief engineer on the project, or whoever is responsible for the project's overall technical excellence, generally chairs the Engineering Review Board. Other members of this board include the project's technical leads who oversee development of the various parts of the project. Collectively, this group should be able to decide whether the change makes technical sense and also what the cost and schedule impacts of the change are.

The second board to approve the change is the Change Control Board (CCB). This board is chaired by whoever is funding the project and is supported by the chief engineer who answers any technical questions raised. The objective of the CCB is to approve the cost and schedule impacts to the project resulting from implementing the change.

Notice that the Engineering Review Board determines whether a change is technically feasible and also determines a cost and schedule impact. The Change Control Board approves the cost and schedule impact.

This two-step approach to change approval ensures that the change is technically sound and affordable. Without this approach, technically questionable changes might be implemented, and there would be no way of controlling cost and schedule issues associated with these changes.

Figure 9-4 shows a flow chart of the two-step change control process described above. As the diagram shows, the ERB considers the change first, followed by the CCB. If the change is approved by the CCB, then the product is taken out of the Configuration Management library, and the change is made.

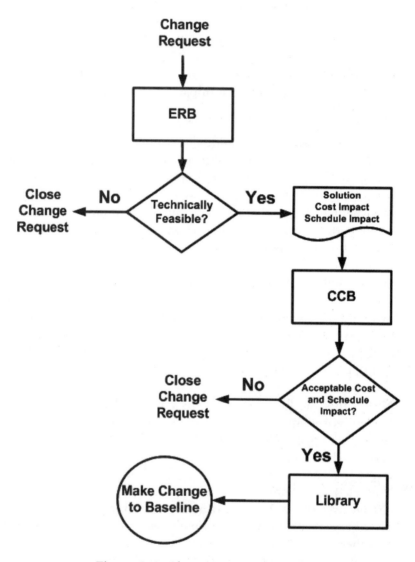

Figure 9-4 Change Control Process

These ideas can be put into a simple example. Consider the hypothetical case of a change request written against an existing system-level requirement upping the requirement to handle peak website traffic by 25 percent.

The first group to view the change is the Engineering Review Board (ERB) chaired by the lead technical person on the program. Other members of the ERB are product leaders for groups with a stake in the outcome of the project.

The ERB reviews the change and decides whether it is technically feasible and, if so, decides what the estimated cost and schedule impacts are.

In this example, the ERB decides the performance increase is technically feasible if more servers are added to the production site. Since the software is being developed in a scaleable architecture, the ERB might decide that there is no impact to the software development effort and that the only cost impact is hardware procurement costs. Further, since the system has not been put into production yet, and since the hardware is expected to be on site within two weeks, the ERB might also decide that there is no schedule impact associated with the change.

As mentioned earlier, the ERB can only approve a change from a technical standpoint. The final approval authority is the Change Control Board (CCB). The CCB is chaired by whoever has the final budget and schedule responsibility for the project.

Based on the result of the ERB, the CCB considers approving the change with the associated cost and schedule impacts. In our example, that means agreeing to buy the extra servers.

The Library Function

A key aspect of a CM process is the CM library where baselined products are kept. Like a traditional library, developers can check in and check out products for use, but not change them. After all, a person can check out a book from the local library, but he or she is not permitted to write in it.

A problem frequently encountered is developers who cannot find critical information. Expensive development personnel should not be wasting time and money looking for anything. Everything they need should be at their fingertips. This is a very easy way to promote productivity and another good reason to set up a Configuration Management library.

As described above, the ERB and CCB approve changes. When changes are approved, the individual responsible for implementing the change is identified and given authority to check the impacted product out of the library with "change" authority. The responsible individual makes the change and checks the changed product back into the library.

A well-run CM library also has a secondary function of notifying everyone that a baseline has changed. It is the responsibility of the development group, based on this notification, to secure the new baseline for future development efforts.

This notification can be done in two ways. Some CM systems use a *pull* notification system, where changes are posted and it is the responsibility of developers and managers to review periodically the posts for changes. An example is a web page that can be viewed by the development team.

The other notification system is based on a *push* system. In this case, change notices are pushed out to the development team. An example of a push system is one based on emails, where the development team receives an email notifying it of a change request to a particular product.

Obviously, push systems are generally more effective at communicating than pull systems since push systems have a higher probability of getting information to those who need it.

Uniquely Identifying Products

The best way to identify a product is with a combination of a unique name and revision number. The important thing is that some predetermined naming convention exists to allow for the unique identification of software products as they are generated.

The revision number must be changed on any product that has been baselined and subsequently changed. Everyone on the development team must be aware of which revision number for a product is the current one.

When a product is first baselined, a good practice is to use the term "Initial" for the release number. After the first change has been approved, the initial release number can be changed to "1.0." Generally, major changes increment the release number by a whole number, such as going from *Revision 1.0* to *Revision 2.0*. Minor changes usually involve incrementing the decimal portion of the release number — for example, going from *Release 1.0* to *Release 1.1*.

Whether a change is considered major or minor depends on the nature of the project and the development organization's culture.

In addition to the revision number, all products should also include an associated date. Every time the revision number is changed, the date must also be changed.

As you can see, an effective Configuration Management system is paramount to controlling changes on a project. All changes have the potential to influence the project's cost, schedule, and technical baselines. Change is not inherently bad if it is controlled and approved. Those are the primary functions a good Configuration Management system provides.

In the next chapter, we will continue our discussion of project development support functions by looking at what it takes to manage software quality.

C H A P T E R   1 0

Managing Quality

A PREVALENT AND SERIOUS cause of cost and schedule impacts is low quality. When quality is lacking, it necessitates rework, and of course, rework impacts both cost and schedule baselines. In this chapter we will see how to implement a rigorous Quality Assurance (QA) program to avoid cost and schedule impacts resulting from poor software quality.

Consider an analogy: in any city there is a criminal element, an element that takes advantage of the system. There are always those who break the rules. These social pariahs would wreak havoc on law abiding citizens if left unchecked. Rule breakers have been a problem ever since people lived together. Over the years, society has developed ways, such as creating and maintaining a police force, to deal with these bad apples.

Software development is similar, especially for enterprises that do not have a long history of developing software. For these companies, software development can turn into the Wild West, characterized as a lawless place run by heroes and those with the quickest draw. Sometimes that is okay, but generally, it is not a good idea to have the Wild West for a software development environment.

That is where Quality Assurance (QA) helps. Think of QA as the police, or the sheriff. Whatever image comes to mind, just remember, QA enforces the rules, and it is rules that make software projects come in on time and on budget.

For most people, thinking about QA as a police force seems strange. In many people's minds, Quality Assurance has to do with building high-quality software. After reading the above introduction, many of you might be wondering what enforcing the rules has to do with producing quality software.

The answer is pretty clear if you give it a moment of thought. A software development organization implements plans and procedures designed to generate quality software. These include generating quality documentation, holding reviews, and using well thought out processes and procedures. All of these activities are meant to guide the development organization down a path that produces the highest quality software possible. The idea is to build software that is reliable, maintainable, and scaleable. In other words, developers want to build quality into the software. See Figure 10-1.

Building in quality is a little different than the more traditional Quality Assurance approach. Traditionally, QA's job is to inspect the final product to ensure that there are no obvious defects. QA inspects a certain percentage of the products coming off the assembly line and determines the overall quality of the batch from statistical analysis, or it finds obvious problems and sends the product back down the

> **Five Keys to Building Highly Reliable Software**
>
> ❑ Follow a well-defined life cycle.
>
> ❑ Follow a well-defined set of procedures.
>
> ❑ Document and control all software products.
>
> ❑ Make heavy use of evaluations.
>
> ❑ Formally review key products.
>
> ❑ Implement a fully functional Quality Assurance group.

Figure 10-1 Five Keys to Building Reliable Software

assembly line for repair. This approach is called inspecting quality into the product.

In software development, it is much better to take a different approach. The idea is to build in quality at every step, starting with the requirements and proceeding through final acceptance testing.

So what does QA have to do with all this? The answer is simple. QA makes sure that all the processes and procedures chosen for the project are followed, and it makes sure that required product reviews are conducted. If the processes dictate that a system requirements specification be developed, QA checks to see that the document was generated. If the process says that the document must be checked for predefined quality attributes, then QA makes sure the inspection takes place.

As you can see, QA personnel are the cops patrolling the development environment. Simply put, QA makes sure that the rules are followed and that the rules include all the steps, templates, and procedures specified for the project.

Of course, testing and system verification are traditional and important roles of the Quality Assurance group, but that is only part of their job. QA starts looking at the way the system is being built from the first day onward.

There is an interesting point to be aware of: QA does not determine the overall *goodness* of a process or a procedure. If a process or procedure is inherently flawed or inefficient, QA's role is still to ensure that it is followed. Its job is to ensure that the process is followed, not to evaluate the overall quality of the process. Of course, QA can be part of the team that generates the processes and procedures in the first place, but once a process or procedure is implemented, whether good or bad, QA is not going to evaluate that process or procedure's inherent value.

For the record, processes and procedures are improved via a process improvement methodology, not by QA direction. This is the cornerstone of Total Quality Management and should be a part of any software development organization's culture. QA might be part of the team implementing the process, but it is no more responsible for the process than any other group.

The same can be said about documentation quality. QA is not going to care whether the document is good or bad in an absolute sense. For example, if requirements are missing or inaccurate, it is not QA's job to make that determination, only to ensure that the document was prepared according to the correct standards and that the right processes were followed to generate the document.

The processes and standards are the means by which it can be certain that all the requirements have been collected. That is why it is so important to have a well-documented set of development processes and procedures. The goodness of the document is determined when it is reviewed during an informal or formal review. Again, QA's job is to ensure that a review takes place if the processes and procedures indicate that one is required.

So now that we know what QA does and does not do, let us take a look at the details of setting up a world-class software Quality Assurance group.

Before continuing, we need to look at a few definitions as applied to Quality Assurance. Take a moment to look over the definitions below so that the rest of the chapter makes sense.

Quality — Quality means that a product meets the requirements levied on it. These requirements might include reliability requirements, maintainability requirements, and scalability requirements. The requirements also include the set of procedures and processes that are followed during development.

Evaluations — Conducting an evaluation means checking that a process, such as the process for collecting requirements, is done according to the procedures defining that process. It also means checking a product to ensure that it follows all applicable templates specified for that product. Products can be any item generated during the development process, such as documentation, reviews, code, test procedures, and test results.

As you will see in the next section, this is a very important concept. However, depending on the size of the development effort, the Quality Assurance organization might consist of only one person, or even one person working part-time on Quality Assurance tasks. The concept of an organization does not imply size, although common sense dictates that the larger the development effort, the larger the QA organization will need to be.

Organizational Ramifications

Software Quality Assurance is, in some respects, a very difficult endeavor. Primarily, QA has the job of calling to task any element of the development effort not in compliance with the enterprise's published standards and procedures.

In many instances, the agenda followed by the Quality Assurance group may be different from that of the development organization. A good example is the tendency of development organizations to cut corners when the schedule or budget gets tight.

These are the times when the Quality Assurance group has to step in and insist that processes and procedures be followed regardless of potential schedule and budget concerns.

To accomplish this, the Quality Assurance group will have to have a reporting channel independent of the development organization's. This ensures that the development organization's management cannot influence the independent objectivity of the Quality Assurance group and also ensures that the Quality Assurance group can make recommendations and submit discrepancy reports in a truly independent and objective manner.

For the Quality Assurance group to have the autonomy required, it must report to the senior manager responsible for the overall project. This is usually the Chief Information Officer or even the president of the organization. Under no circumstances should the Quality Assurance organization report to the development organization.

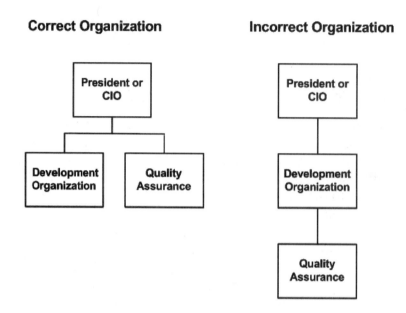

Figure 10-2 Different Quality Assurance Organizations

As Figure 10-2 shows, the ideal situation is an organization where the Quality Assurance group reports directly to the president. In many cases this reporting is a hard-line on the company's organization chart.

Using Evaluations to Increase Quality

Making sure that processes and procedures are followed is easily accomplished by chartering the QA organization to perform evaluations. At a minimum, the QA organization should perform evaluations to ensure that the development effort follows the procedures, plans, and specifications assigned to the project. Once the software has been coded and is ready for testing or production, QA should also evaluate that the correct version of the software is being used in the tests or being put into production.

These four types of evaluations cover all significant aspects of the development effort. In some instances, other evaluations might be required, such as an evaluation of the Configuration Management procedures or even the QA procedures. Of course, in the latter case, an independent organization should perform the evaluation.

Evaluations for Procedural Compliance

Procedures and policies define what must be done. Often, with hectic development schedules and tight budgets, key steps in a procedure may be skipped either inadvertently or deliberately. In either event, it is QA's responsibility to evaluate the development effort to determine whether all the applicable procedures are being followed. See Figure 10-3.

Of course, this requires that the QA organization be very familiar with all the procedures applicable to the project.

QA evaluations are ongoing with an emphasis on the procedures pertaining to the current life-cycle phase. In other words, it is unlikely that the QA group would spend much time making sure that the project is in compliance with a detailed planning procedure when the project is in the testing phase.

Further, on some projects, certain procedures or steps in a procedure might not be applicable. In cases such as this, it should be determined ahead of time that certain procedures are not applicable, and a written waiver should be generated by the appropriate parties documenting the steps waived.

There are many cases where parts of processes or procedures are ignored when it comes time to exe-

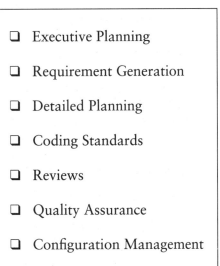

❑ Executive Planning

❑ Requirement Generation

❑ Detailed Planning

❑ Coding Standards

❑ Reviews

❑ Quality Assurance

❑ Configuration Management

Figure 10-3 Typical Procedures Used for Software Development

cute them. Certainly this is unacceptable, unless it has been predetermined that these parts are not required.

Evaluations for Plan Compliance

Generally, there are several plans that form the basis of a well-run software development effort. These plans contain details on how certain activities such as Configuration Management are conducted on the development effort. In general, most projects include key plans such as a Project Plan, the Quality Assurance Plan, and the Configuration Management Plan.

Each of these plans covers important activities required to produce truly world-class software.

The QA organization's responsibility with regard to these plans is twofold. First, the QA organization must ensure that each plan is written according to the template for that plan. A template is nothing more than a predefined outline for a plan specifying what is contained in the plan and in what order this material should be presented. Templates simplify writing documents by specifying important content. By using a template, technical writers and software developers can supply the details for each paragraph instead of having to think up the content and organization of the document. This approach saves time and money.

Second, QA must determine that the plan is actually being followed. For example, if the Software Development Plan specifies the project schedule be updated on a weekly basis, QA verifies that this is indeed done.

Evaluation for Project Specifications Compliance

Every project should be built according to a detailed set of specifications, including requirement and design specifications. Failure to do this results in needless schedule and cost impacts.

For example, QA's role with respect to the requirements specification is threefold. First, QA must ensure that the requirements specification was written according to the correct template. Second, and more important, QA should make sure that the flow down of requirements from higher-level specifications to lower-level specifications is correct. Third, QA makes sure that a test methodology is specified for each requirement.

Notice in this discussion that it is not QA's role to come up with requirements. That is the job of the systems analyst. Nor is it the job of QA to determine the quality of the requirements. This is accomplished at requirement reviews or requirement walk-throughs.

In many cases, the number of requirements may be very large. In this case, QA probably does not have the resources and time to review every requirement. In these situations, QA can select a representative set of requirements for evaluation.

QA's role with respect to requirements validation is to ensure that sufficient test procedures are written to test the requirements adequately. The second aspect of QA's role in requirements validation is to observe that the actual tests are conducted according to the test procedures. This does not imply that the QA group actually performs the testing. In world-class development organizations, an independent test group, not QA, usually conducts formal acceptance testing.

Many development organizations define their QA organization as the group that performs formal testing. There are several problems with this approach. First, as noted above, verifying requirements is only a small part of the total QA organization's responsibilities. Enterprises that rely on their QA organization for testing and nothing more are missing the most important aspect of the QA group's responsibility, namely to ensure that quality is built into the system, not just tested into the system at delivery time.

The second problem with chartering a QA organization as the group performing formal testing is that it requires the QA group be technically competent with testing techniques. Testing is a complicated art requiring a specialized set of skills and training. Good testers must be very familiar with the technical content of the product that they are testing and also have a good foundation in the languages and tools used to develop the product. Forcing your QA organization into this role requires a different skill mix than developing a QA organization based on the concept of evaluations of important quality producing procedures.

The argument for using the QA group to conduct testing is that developers cannot be trusted to do their own testing. This is valid. It is the old fox in the hen house argument. However, when the watchful eye of the QA organization monitors the testers, they can no longer cut corners or stretch testing results from unfavorable to acceptable.

If, for some reason, the developers are not to be trusted with testing, then a stand-alone test organization should be formed. In most companies this group is referred to as an IV and V group, which stands for Independent Verification and Validation. Using an IV and V group has many merits, including giving you the ability to collect into one group talented testers who can span multiple projects with their skill base. It also frees up the developers to focus on correcting problems during the end phase of the project when the IV and V group takes over testing.

Evaluations for Correct Software Versioning

The process of developing software is iterative by nature. This is especially true during the testing of the software when bugs are discovered and corrected. Every time software is modified, a new version of the software is created. Versions must be tracked so that when it comes time to put the system into production, the production version is the same as the last software version tested.

It is also important to note that there are three times when versioning is crucial. The first is before the start of factory acceptance testing. For this activity to be successful, a very careful inventory of the software versions must be made. During factory acceptance testing, bugs can be discovered and corrected. The corrected software is subjected to regression tests. Again, it is very important to ensure that the correct version of software is being tested. Factory acceptance testing is explained in Chapter 11, "Testing."

The second time when versioning is very important is during site acceptance testing. Although the instances of bugs at this point are significantly lower, in all probability some will still be found. As was the case during factory acceptance testing, the bugs must be corrected and a new version of the software generated for regression testing. Site acceptance testing is also explained in Chapter 11.

Finally, versioning is very important when the software becomes operational. The correct version of the software must be installed. From this point forward, versioning continues to be important, as users will no doubt find a few remaining bugs, and the software will undoubtedly be enhanced. It is important to install the correct version of the software and be able to go back to a previous working version in the event that something goes seriously awry.

Correcting Problems Discovered During Evaluations

After reading the above description of the duties of the QA organization, you may be thinking that the QA group is bound to find something. The truth is, they will find deficiencies — some of which will be accidental and others not. In either case, there must be some method to document the deficiency and to ensure that corrective action is taken. This is the realm of the corrective action process discussed next.

When QA finds a deficiency, it writes a deficiency report. The report can be fairly straightforward and should describe the deficiency in detail. It should also describe how the deficiency is going to be corrected, who is responsible for correcting the deficiency, and when the deficiency is going to be fixed.

Action items and deficiency reports have a habit of getting lost or, equally problematic, being totally ignored. To prevent this from happening, a log of all deficiency reports must be maintained. This log should be readily available, especially to management.

It is a simple matter to generate a report on a weekly or monthly basis that lists all open discrepancies. This report can then be sent to whomever has the authority to get the deficiency closed. The report can also be sent to all project managers and senior management.

Conducting Evaluations

Earlier, the concept of an evaluation was discussed. Now, we will take a little time to provide easy-to-follow-guidelines for conducting evaluations.

Before we go into detail, realize that there is an important difference between the implementation of quality in the software industry as opposed to other industries. In many industries, quality is implemented by testing the final product. That approach does not work well for software. The fact is, quality cannot be guaranteed through testing alone. Instead, software quality must be built into the product at each phase of the life cycle. Quality is typically achieved by following well defined processes.

The whole idea of "building in" quality as opposed to simply testing a finished product becomes clearer if you consider the case of requirements. A good example of a requirements evaluation is the system requirements review. If, during the review, no new requirements are identified, the design and coding phase can commence with the completed set of requirements. On the other hand, if the review (i.e., an evaluation) is not done, requirements might be missed, resulting in significant rework downstream, or worse, a product that does not work. In this example, having the review not only increases quality, but also decreases cost and schedule impacts by identifying deficiencies much earlier in the life cycle, when corrective action is much less costly to implement.

Another example of an evaluation is a code review. During this review, several criteria can be used to increase the overall quality of the code. These include ensuring that the code adheres to published standards, such as coding standards and naming conventions, as well as inspecting the code for technical correctness.

This includes making sure that all the logic is correct and ensuring that the code implements published interfaces correctly.

In all cases, evaluations should be thought of as another form of testing. Developers and managers can readily recognize the advantages of this approach since evaluations are inexpensive and much quicker to conduct than formal testing. Further, since evaluations occur throughout the life cycle, mistakes caught during an evaluation translate into huge cost savings downstream. Contrast that to the cost associated with catching the mistakes during formal testing.

Finally, consider the fact that world-class software development organizations strive to produce software with zero defects at delivery time. This is very hard to accomplish. Evaluations, coupled with code reuse and rigorous testing, are the three most promising approaches to achieving that goal.

Before we go any further, we need to address a subject debated widely. Should management be present during evaluations?

On the one hand, many managers want to attend evaluations because they find these meetings informative. In this case, it is hard to keep management out, although evaluations are not the correct place to "get smart." As a matter of fact, this is the last place you want people to become informed on the project. People at evaluations are supposed to know what is going on so that they can contribute effectively to the evaluation.

On the other hand, there is a widespread school of thought that managers should not be present at evaluations, because if the evaluation is working correctly, it often highlights deficiencies in the inspected product. Many developers do not want management present when their work is scrutinized and, to some extent, criticized.

Where the correct answer lies is up to you and your corporate culture. As a general rule, if your corporate environment is confrontational and there is a case of class warfare going on between management and developers, then banning management from the evaluations is probably the best course of action.

However, if the corporate environment views management as an important team member, then include management in evaluations. The rationale here is that the more eyes that see a product, the more likely that deficiencies will be identified. Also, this is a good place for management to identify systemic problems. If the same issues continually pop up at review after review, it probably indicates that management needs to fix some underlying problem, such as compressed schedules or resource problems existing on the project.

General Evaluation Criteria

Evaluations can and should be conducted on all software products prior to release. For the sake of this discussion, software products include but are not limited to:

❏ System requirements specifications

❏ System design documents

❏ Software Requirements Specifications

❏ Configuration Item design documents

❏ Configuration Item code

❏ Test plans

❏ Test procedures

We will consider each in turn.

Evaluating System Requirements Specifications

The purpose of the system requirements evaluation is to ensure that the system-level requirements are complete, accurate, and equally important, testable.

Of the three criteria, perhaps the most important is to ensure that all the system requirements have been identified. It does not take a lot of common sense to realize that if the project progresses past the system analysis phase without all of the system-level requirements being identified, then the end result will be a lot of rework. Naturally, this causes cost and schedule overruns.

The best way to ensure requirement completeness is to make sure the correct subject matter experts evaluate the requirements. It is equally important that these subject matter experts realize the importance of the evaluation and also that the consequence of not taking the evaluation seriously could lead to large cost and schedule impacts.

A second aspect of the evaluation is to ensure that all of the requirements are testable. For example, requirements such as "The system shall be easy to use," should be rewritten with more meaningful and testable verbiage. Another aspect of testability is ambiguity. A requirement that is even slightly ambiguous needs to be rewritten, since it will not only cause problems during development, but also during testing.

Remember, testing takes time, and the clearer and more testable the system-level requirements are, the easier and cheaper testing will be. Do not clutter up downstream efforts with mistakes generated early in the project. The requirements evaluation is the place to catch these types of mistakes, before they are propagated through the entire life cycle.

A third category to focus on when evaluating system-level requirements is verifying that the requirements are feasible. Remember, nothing is impossible if you do not have to do it yourself. Some aspects of a development effort may be beyond the means of the enterprise's development organization. When these types of requirements are identified, they either have to be dropped, given to a third party for implementation, or the current organization must hire new personnel capable of implementing them. This type of situation is particularly likely if the requirement has to be implemented with new technology or technology requiring skill mixes not currently available.

Requirements evaluations are a good place to decide whether a requirement is necessary or not. Often, requirements get listed early in the project only to be deleted later when it is realized that they are either not needed or that the functionality is actually covered elsewhere. Removing these duplicate requirements upfront reduces development costs and leads to a much cleaner design. Further, some requirements might be dropped simply because what seemed like a good idea in the beginning no longer seems like such a good idea.

Finally, requirements evaluations should focus on identifying conflicting requirements. Implementing one requirement may be totally contradictory to implementing another in the requirements specification. Sometimes the conflict is obvious, other times it takes a sharp eye to spot it.

Requirements evaluations are conducted periodically as blocks of requirements are completed, or on a prescheduled basis such as weekly.

On a final note, do not confuse requirements evaluations with requirements reviews. Requirements evaluations are working-level meetings with the sole purpose of ensuring that the requirements are complete, testable, doable, and do not conflict with other requirements. Requirements evaluations are designed to ensure the overall quality of the requirements before design and implementation phases are started.

Requirements reviews, on the other hand, are designed to get end users and stakeholders to agree that the requirements accurately reflect what they want. Requirements reviews should never be used to catch lower-level issues such as ambiguity or testability. These should have been discovered and corrected long before the requirements review.

Evaluating System Design Documents

It goes without saying that getting the system design correct goes a long way toward completing the project on time and on budget. Since all activities that come later are intimately dependent on the design, it is very important that the team make sure that the design is correct.

When inspecting the design, consider the following criteria:

❑   Is the design maintainable?

❑   Is the design scalable?

❑   Does the design promote reliability?

Maintainability
The importance of maintainability cannot be emphasized enough. The equation,

Revenues - Expenses = Profits

shows that this is true. Software by its nature should increase revenues either directly, by contributing to sales, or indirectly, by means such as increasing employee productivity.

Software systems can also increase expenses, and those expenses can be summarized in one word, "maintainability." The upshot is that maintainable software is less expensive to upgrade and fix than less maintainable software. Lower expenses translate directly into higher corporate profits. The moral of the story is to build maintainable software and save money later.

Do not let time-to-market factors cloud the issue. Many companies make the serious mistake of developing software in a hurry to hit some perceived time-to-market requirement. Perhaps the time-to-market requirement is really an issue, but many times it is not.

In any event, do not sacrifice maintainability for time-to-market. Perhaps you can get the product out a couple of months earlier, but seriously consider the fact that, in many cases, the product will be operational for years. The extra costs associated with maintaining a poorly written system far outweigh the small advantages the early time-to-market brought.

Scalability

Scalability is related to maintainability. Scalability implies that the software can be easily modified to accommodate growth. This generally means more people using the system in a given time period with no degradation of performance.

Typically, software systems are sized for a certain load with an associated performance. However, in this brave new cyber world, it is very difficult to predict what that load will be in six months and probably impossible to predict what it will be in two or three years. Therefore, it is very important to design the final product with performance growth in mind.

Reliability

Software systems should behave in a predictable manner and without significant bugs. This is the whole story behind reliability.

We have identified techniques throughout this book that contribute to highly reliable software. These include:

❑ Correctly specifying the requirements

❑ Employing a modular design

❑ Implementing a three-level testing approach

❑ Inspecting the design for reliability

Practice these evaluation approaches religiously and you will be well on the way to building more reliable software.

Evaluating Software Requirements Specifications

The same objectives that applied to the system requirements evaluations apply to the lower-level software requirements evaluations. Software requirements are system requirements that have been further defined down to a level that can be turned over to a developer for implementation. Software requirements are allocated to specific Configuration Items. This means there can be multiple software requirements evaluations, that is, one or more for each Configuration Item.

Some unique items to focus on with software requirements are:

❑ **Traceability** — Is the requirement traceable to a system requirement?

❑ **Allocation** — Does the requirement really belong with the current Configuration Item, or should it be reassigned to another?

❑ **Ambiguity** — Is the requirement unambiguous?

❑ **Testability** — Are all the requirements testable?

We consider each of the above criteria in more detail next.

Traceability
Every CI or subsystem requirement must trace to a higher-level system requirement. This ensures that only the software that is actually required is built. This is important because every requirement generates a huge development expense as software is designed, coded, and tested. Weeding out unnecessary requirements upfront is one simple way to cut cost. Furthermore, the larger the code base, the more likely it is to have bugs. Reducing the number of requirements cuts down on the code size, which directly promotes greater product reliability.

If software requirements are showing up that do not trace to the system requirements, one of two things is happening. First, it could be that the team is starting to build software that is not actually required, or second, that the system requirements are not complete.

In the first case, unnecessary requirements should be eliminated at once. If, on the other hand, the team decides that a large portion of the system requirements is missing, effort on the software requirements should be stopped, and the system specification should be revisited and completed.

Allocation

Sometimes during the system analysis and design phase, a requirement is incorrectly allocated to a Configuration Item. As the design evolves and the requirements are clarified, it will often become apparent that a certain requirement should really be allocated to another Configuration Item.

Catching bad allocations early will contribute greatly to a cleaner design. Better designs are easier to code and test and yield considerable cost savings during the development and testing phases of the project. In addition, clean designs are always more maintainable, yielding significant cost savings after the system goes into operation.

Ambiguity

Ambiguity has the potential to cause several major and time consuming problems. First, ambiguous requirements squander developers' time as they struggle to figure out what the requirement actually means.

Unambiguous requirements allow the developers to hit the pavement running. Debating what a requirement means is a needless waste of time and something well-run evaluations will eliminate.

Second, and more seriously, ambiguous requirements can cause serious problems later in the project after a lot of code is developed and tested. Stakeholders using the completed product will determine that the system is not working as expected. This situation can have devastating implications for future cost and schedule growth.

Testability

Be sure that all the requirements are testable. Examples of requirements that are not testable are those containing adjectives such as "fast" or "easy to use." Obviously, these terms mean different things to different people.

Evaluating Configuration Item Design Documents

There are eight major items to look for when conducting a Configuration Item design evaluation. They are:

❑ **Traceability** — Are all the requirements allocated to the Configuration Item implemented?

❑ **Modularity** — Is the design modular?

❑ **Maintainability** — Is the design maintainable?

❑ **Reliability** — Is the design inherently reliable?

❑ **Scalability** — Is the design scaleable?

❑ **Design optimization** — Are there better designs?

❑ **Interface fidelity** — Are all interfaces implemented correctly?

❑ **Testability** — Are all the functions testable?

Evaluating Code

This is perhaps the easiest of all the evaluations to conduct. Evaluating code simply means reviewing the code to verify that it follows the accepted coding and naming standards on the project. This also includes database conventions.

The following standards are usually applied during code evaluations:

❑ **Language coding standards** — Unique for each language implemented. These generally cover naming, formatting, and commenting guidelines.

❑ **Scripting standards** — Cover coding and naming standards for scripting languages. Also provide guidance on selecting server-side processing versus client-side processing.

❏ **HTML standards** — Cover naming and formatting of HTML code.

❏ **Database standards** — Cover naming and coding standards for database objects such as stored procedures and tables.

Why are coding standards important? First, well thought out coding standards are designed to make coding easier and to eliminate errors. For example, your coding standards might specify that loops cannot be nested more than three deep. Superficially, this might not seem like much of a big deal, but when you consider how difficult it is to test a set of nested loops that go more than three deep, you can understand the logic and wisdom of this standard.

Second, if it follows accepted coding standards, the code will be easier to maintain in the future. As we have seen, anything that reduces maintenance cost is a good thing.

Strict adherence to coding and naming conventions means that new employees can more readily maintain existing code long after the original developers have moved on. If the enterprise does not have an accepted set of coding and naming conventions, the first thing to do is to stop everything and get a set. Coding standards are not hard to develop and are even easier to find in books and on the Internet.

Evaluating Test Plans and Procedures

The final items to evaluate are the test plans and procedures. It is easier to look over test procedures and spot mistakes than to be in the middle of a test scenario and find out that the testers are not testing what they should be testing.

When evaluating test procedures, make sure that they cover all the requirements at the system, subsystem, and Configuration Item levels.

Also make sure the procedures are easy to follow, and specify the expected result.

Be sure that the Quality Assurance (QA) group is familiar with the test procedures and can witness the test based on the procedures. We cover testing in much more detail in the next chapter.

Now that we have seen what types of things we should look for in the evaluations, the next step is to turn our attention to the details of setting up and documenting a product evaluation.

How to Conduct an Evaluation

Conducting a successful evaluation, regardless of the type, involves completing the following steps:

❑ Coordinating the evaluation

❑ Conducting the evaluation

Coordinating the Evaluation

Prior to conducting an evaluation, it is important that the material to be reviewed is given to everyone involved. This is accomplished via the following steps:

Determine Evaluation Attendees
Evaluation attendees should consist of individuals familiar enough with the material to be able to provide constructive criticism. These attendees include other personnel working on similar parts of the project and those building interfaces with the product being evaluated.

Notify Attendees of the Date and Time of the Evaluation
The longer the attendees have to review the material, the better the job of reviewing they will do. In general, notifications should be provided at least two working days prior to the actual evaluation. These notifications give evaluation participants time to review the material and also increase the probability that the members will attend. Scheduling evaluations at the 11th hour is not a good strategy and will result in low-quality evaluations because no one will have had time to review the material. Also, many participants will have schedule conflicts.

Provide Attendees with the Material To Be Inspected

It is important to provide the attendees with the material to be evaluated or at least to indicate where it can be found. Be sure to make clear the parts of the material that are subject to evaluation. In some cases, this is easier to do by providing the material in soft copy. Other times it is easier to conduct the evaluation when everyone has a hard copy.

Appoint a Note Taker

There are always action items and issues resulting from evaluations. Someone has to record these for future action. The person appointed should be familiar with the material being evaluated. If the meeting is in a conference room without a PC, use a laptop. It makes everything much easier, including distributing the minutes after the meeting is over.

Appoint an Evaluation Leader

The evaluation leader has the job of running the evaluation in an orderly fashion. The evaluation leader also has the task of making sure that the evaluation stays focused and does not deviate to unrelated topics. Finally, the evaluation leader must make sure that the meeting starts and stops on time.

Guidelines for Conducting the Evaluation

Evaluations should be non-confrontational. This means the product, not the developer of the product, should be scrutinized. True issues should be identified and an action plan formulated for the resolution of these issues.

The note taker should record all issues and document who is responsible for closing the issues. They should record a due date for completion of action items. All action items should be included as part of the minutes, which are published immediately after the evaluation. Everyone who participated in the evaluation receives a copy of the minutes. Minutes should also be maintained for historical purposes in the CM library.

All personnel participating in the evaluation must come prepared to participate and contribute. With that said, it is important to remember that evaluations are not meant to educate peripheral members of the team about a particular product. This is not an efficient method of providing information. Do not use evaluations as a means of bringing others up to speed on the functions and purpose of a product because it wastes time and dilutes the overall effectiveness of the evaluation.

If members of management are present, they should contribute as value-adding members, not as supervisors looking for employee performance appraisal material. Management should focus on the managerial issues holding the team up and not on second guessing the technical competence of those developing the products. Management should manage, not develop software.

However, there are true management issues that may come to light at product reviews. For example, the review might indicate that the requirements are not complete. This could become a management issue if the underlying reason is the lack of personnel. Management's role in this situation is to figure out how to staff the project most effectively.

The meeting leader must maintain the overall focus and objectives of the evaluation. This includes not only keeping the team on track, but also making sure that discussions pertaining to an item are not unduly long. Some issues might require extensive consultation, and these matters should be taken offline with the appropriate team members participating. In the event that an item is scheduled for further review, an action item should be taken specifying when and where the offline meeting is to occur and what the expected outcome is. Also note how the meeting's results will be communicated back to the development staff.

The evaluation team leader must also make sure that matters not directly related to the evaluation are not discussed. People get distracted and move off topic at meetings. This is human nature and must be recognized and dealt with appropriately. Peripheral discussions are not only disruptive, but also unduly lengthen meetings, wasting the precious time of other team members not directly involved with the side issue being discussed.

As a general rule, evaluations should be short. Anything over an hour is too long, except under unusual circumstances. Team members do not want to spend more than an hour away from other tasks. Also, meetings lasting over an hour are probably not efficient, as team members' minds start wandering.

When an evaluation will take more than an hour — for instance, when reviewing system requirements — multiple evaluations covering parts of the completed product should be scheduled. This shortens the time of each evaluation and generally increases the quality of the evaluations.

Evaluations Versus Formal Reviews

With all of the discussion on evaluation, you might be wondering what the differences between an evaluation and a formal review are. Evaluations and formal reviews are distinct and different in terms of the scope and the objectives of each. They should not be confused.

Evaluations are ongoing aspects of the analysis, design, coding, and testing processes and are used to ensure the overall quality of a product, such as the code or a requirements specification, prior to baseline and release.

Evaluations are held and attended by the development team and, in some cases, with a subset of the stakeholders. Evaluations are often done incrementally as parts of a product are completed, as opposed to a review of the completed product.

Formal reviews, on the other hand, are conducted once for each product, at the end of the development phase for that product. They are usually not incremental.

Whereas the development team, for the sake of product quality, conducts evaluations, formal reviews are more often conducted with the end user to get approval to continue on with the next phase of the project. For example, in the case of a system requirements specification, the finished specification may be formally reviewed with subject matter experts to get their signoff before design and coding start.

Formal reviews are used to establish baselines. Baselines are points from which changes are formally controlled. Without formal reviews, users and stakeholders could continue to change their minds on a variety of issues without facing the cost and schedule impacts associated with these changes. Once a baseline is established, all changes are made with the associated cost and schedule impacts factored into the change. This was discussed in Chapter 9.

Formal reviews have a purpose, as do evaluations. Use each to your advantage and your end product will have much higher quality.

Now that you understand how a well-structured Quality Assurance organization can help your project come in on time and on budget, we can turn our attention to the last subject, which is testing. Testing is a subset of Quality Assurance, but is covered separately in the next chapter.

CHAPTER 11

Testing

IN ADDITION TO HAVING a QA organization and conducting evaluations, another aspect of a world-class Quality Assurance program is using a first-rate test program. We complete our discussion of quality by covering this important concept next.

It does not matter how good the design or coding is if the software does not work exactly as expected, and we all know that expectations can vary significantly. So how do you make sure that your completed software system meets expectations, and, at the same time, works? The answer: you write good test plans and test procedures.

Before going into the details, consider the following definitions:

❑ **Test plan** — A document answering the *who, what, when,* and *where* questions about system testing. Notice the "how" part is where test procedures come into play.

❑ **Test procedure** — A document answering the *"how"* questions about system testing.

The distinction between the two is important, since there are a number of organizational and management issues associated with testing that many organizations ignore. These are things that have to be addressed at some time and, by ignoring them, you risk unnecessary delays that can be easily avoided with a little thought upfront. This is why a test plan is so important.

A test procedure is what most people think about when they think of testing. It covers details about how the software will be tested and what the test results should look like. In the case of tests that generate a large volume of data, the test procedures might even contain sections on data reduction. The easiest way to think about it is that the test procedure is a technical document, whereas the test plan is more of a management document.

Types of Testing

Regardless of the complexity of your project, you should always plan on conducting the following tests:

❏ Development testing

❏ Factory testing

❏ Site testing

Development Testing

Developers perform development testing as they finish coding the software. The reasons behind development testing are to find and fix bugs and to ensure that the software does not have logic errors. This includes the usual list of culprits, such as loops and interfaces that do not work correctly. Development testing is the time to catch as many bugs as possible.

Successful development testing makes factory testing and site testing go much more smoothly because logic errors have already been caught and corrected prior to these later phases of testing, which focus on making sure that the system meets all requirements.

Factory Testing

The term "factory testing" refers to the fact that the software is being tested where it was built (at the software factory if you will) and not on the production servers. Factory testing is the first step of acceptance testing. Acceptance testing, as the name implies, is a formal level of testing designed to show that the software meets all of the requirements and can be "accepted" for production.

Notice that the definition of factory testing does not include making sure that the logic behind the software works. This should have been done during the development testing described above.

If you recall from Chapter 6, "Determining the Development Organization and Allocating Budget," a system can consist of subsystems and Configuration Items. In the case of subsystems, each subsystem has its own requirements specification, as does each Configuration Item. This implies that there can be three levels of factory testing, as shown in Figure 11-1 below.

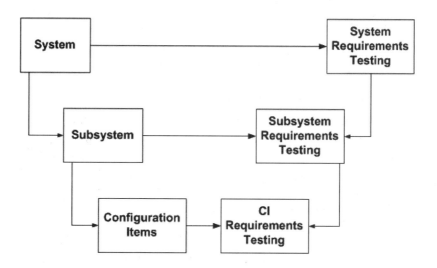

Figure 11-1 Levels of Factory Testing

Therefore, the first thing to go through factory testing is the Configuration Items, to make sure that each Configuration Item meets all the requirements allocated to it.

After the Configuration Items have been tested, the next step is to test the subsystems. At this point, you might be wondering why subsystems must be tested if the Configuration Items were adequately tested.

The reason is to make sure that all of the Configuration Items work together. In other words, each Configuration Item might work just fine by itself, but when you hook them up to make the subsystem, they may not interface with each other correctly. This problem can only be caught with a set of test procedures dedicated to testing the integrated Configuration Items.

The system-level testing is designed to demonstrate that the subsystems work together correctly. This actually means making sure that the software associated with CIs in one subsystem interfaces correctly with CIs in other subsystems.

Testing Environment

A key requirement for factory testing is to create a factory test environment that looks and feels exactly like the operational environment. This step is extremely important. Everything about the factory test environment should be exactly the same as the production environment, including the servers and the software running on them. If this rule is not followed, there is a chance that software that has been factory tested successfully might not work as expected when loaded onto the production hardware.

Site Testing

This next level of testing is called site testing because the software is being tested on the production hardware (that is the operational *site*).

Once the software has completed factory testing and has been moved to the operational environment, a subset of the factory test procedures must be run to ensure that the software is installed correctly. This is called site testing. Generally, for site testing, running a subset of the factory test procedures is all that is required since factory testing has been done in an environment similar to the operational site.

Once it has been determined that the software has been installed correctly, a quick end-to-end regression test can be run to confirm that all functionality has been implemented and works correctly in the production environment.

It is important to have a documented procedure for running regression tests, because once the system goes into operation, the regression tests must be run every time the system is upgraded or fixed. In many cases, this is a fairly common occurrence, so a regression test that is not only complete and accurate, but also quick to run, is an excellent goal.

The Relationship Between Acceptance Testing and Development Testing

The methodology described above explains three levels of testing. The first level of testing, development testing, is focused on finding bugs and making sure that all elements of the software interface correctly. This type of testing has often been referred to as *unit testing*.

Factory testing, on the other hand, is concerned with making sure that the software meets all the requirements specified in the requirements specifications. This is an entirely different focus from development testing, which is targeted at finding bugs. The two versions of testing are required to ensure that bugs are caught and that the system meets all the requirements.

Having a bug-free system that does not meet requirements is not satisfactory. Neither is having a system that meets the requirements but is buggy.

Finally, site testing is needed to ensure that no issues arise from installing the new software on the production hardware.

It is assumed that the reader is familiar with testing techniques associated with development testing, and so this subject will not be discussed any further in this book. Hereafter, we will concern ourselves with learning how to complete factory and site testing successfully.

Types of Factory/Site Tests

When we speak about how requirements are tested, either during factory or site testing, we are actually referring to one of four testing techniques. These are:

❑ Demonstration

❑ Inspection

❑ Analysis

❑ Test

Demonstration

As the name implies, demonstration is a form of testing that demonstrates a requirement has been met.

Consider, for example, an interface requirement that specifies that the web interface shall have fields for the customer's name, credit card number, and expiration date.

Obviously, the easiest way to show that this requirement has been met is simply to bring up the web page and *demonstrate* that the required fields are present. The success criteria for this option are that the fields exist, which can easily be demonstrated.

The above example shows that demonstration is appropriate for most types of interface requirements, including output requirements, such as reports. Most users specify the requirements for a report by saying, "make it look like this." Obviously, demonstrating to the end users that the report looks the way they wanted it most easily tests this type of requirement.

In general, demonstration is the easiest test method to use and, in many cases, suffices.

Inspection

Inspection means that part of the system, such as the code, is inspected to validate that it meets a requirement. For example, suppose that for maintainability reasons, there is a requirement that objects be written in Java. Obviously, the easiest way to verify this requirement is simply to take a look at the code and make sure that it is written in Java.

Another example might consist of a system where there is a requirement that the system use a specific version of a hardware driver. Again, the easiest way to verify this requirement is simply to inspect that the correct version of the driver was installed.

Inspection often involves looking at parts of the system and then extrapolating for the entire system. Considering the example given above — that the software must be written in Java — it is unlikely that all the code would be inspected for compliance. Instead, parts of the code would be selected and inspected and the results extrapolated to the rest of the code.

Inspection, as a test method, has limited uses and will generally not show up often in most test documents.

Analysis

Analysis can be a complicated test method since it involves developing more sophisticated data evaluation methods. Analysis is used when the data generated by a test is analyzed to prove that a requirement was met. This usually means that a fairly large amount of data is generated and collected. In cases such as this, data reduction software is needed to reduce the volume of data into meaningful results, such as graphs and values resulting from statistical analyses.

Often, performance requirements, such as response time under maximum load, cannot be duplicated in the test environment. When this is true, the performance data generated during the testing phase must be extrapolated to approximate the actual performance under operational loads. This is a good example of analysis.

Test

Test is the most generic of the four test methods. Test could be inspection or demonstration, but generally implies a more involved procedure than simply inspecting some aspect of the system for compliance or demonstrating some feature of the system for compliance.

Generally, test requires a set of steps to verify a requirement. These steps form the basis of a test procedure and are usually more involved than simple inspection or demonstration.

However, in many cases, both demonstration and inspection are required for a test, so the distinction between these test methods can be blurred somewhat. As a general rule, if the test requires a set of steps for completion, the test method can be considered "test" as opposed to one of the other methods.

Assigning Test Methods to Requirements

Every requirement must have a test method assigned to it. This is very important for several reasons.

First, having a test method assigned to each requirement forms a test baseline that can be reviewed. Stakeholders, including developers, can conduct what is known as a Test Readiness Review (TRR) to review the adequacy of the testing approach.

Second, having a test method assigned to a requirement and successfully completing the associated test proves that the system correctly implemented that requirement.

Third, by successfully testing all of the requirements, developers and managers can close the development effort. This does not mean that there will not be further enhancements, but it does mean that the original scope of the project is complete. Often, this step is very important from a contractual standpoint.

Test Plans

Test plans are written for a wide range of products. Sometimes, a test plan will be written for a stand-alone system, but more often it is written to cover a system that must be integrated into an environment containing legacy systems. For this reason, it is important to be specific about the software to which the plan applies.

As shown in Figure 11-2, test plans can be written for all levels of the system

Many new systems interface with other legacy systems. It is important to specify how those interfaces are tested. For example, a question such as, "Who is responsible for testing each side of the interface?" has to be answered in the test plan.

Generally, test plans include the following sections:

❏ Test sites

❏ Test items

❏ Required hardware

❏ Participating organizations

❏ Testing times

❏ Tests to perform

❏ Test results and analysis

❏ Test schedules

❏ Requirement traceability

We will cover each in detail below.

❏ *System Test Plans* — Describe how the system requirements will be testeed.

❏ *Subsytem Test Plans* — Describe how each subsystem will be tested.

❏ *Configuration Item Test Plans* — Describe how each configuration item will be tested.

Figure 11-2
Types of Test Plans

Test Sites

This section identifies the test sites used for testing. For example, are the tests conducted in the development shop or at some other location, such as an operations site?

If the software is tested at the operations center, the managers of the center must be informed ahead of time. No doubt they will have to make allowances in the day-to-day operations of the center to accommodate the testing. They must plan for new software drops and must know ahead of time which parts of the legacy operations are impacted most heavily.

In the case where multiple test plans are needed — for example, when several software programs are involved — the relationship between the different test plans must be specified. This ensures that there is no confusion as to the scope of the testing activity spelled out in the test plans.

Test Items

It is necessary to identify the software to be tested at each site. This is particularly important for distributed systems and systems that are spread over more than one computer in multiple locations.

Do not forget to include all the support software required for the test. On complicated systems, this list can be quite lengthy and would include items such as:

❑ Data generation software

❑ Stubs

❑ Simulators

❑ Data reduction software

❑ Legacy software

Data Generation Software

In many cases, extensive data must be generated prior to the start of testing. For example, users, products, and catalogs might have to be created before a test is run. Sometimes a very large amount of data has to be generated to simulate performance requirements. This might entail running special software to create the data.

Stubs

Stubs are small software programs simulating real-world things like other software programs. Often, in a testing environment, certain parts of the system are "stubbed out" so that the test can be run without impacting anything. A good example is to stub out a legacy system to which the new system interfaces. Stubs are removed once it is determined that the new system is stable and will not affect the legacy system.

Simulators

Simulators are like stubs but are more complicated. Simulators, as the term implies, simulate some aspect of the system. A good example of a simulator is a piece of software that generates hundreds of simulated orders a minute to approximate the load on a system during peak usage.

Data Reduction Software

Data reduction software is traditionally employed heavily in scientific applications where the new system generates a great deal of data to be evaluated. Sometimes, special software is needed to sort through raw data to verify that the new system runs correctly.

For a system, data reduction software might be as simple as a package that graphs performance as a percent of load. Although simple, this example shows that in many cases data reduction software is required in some form or another.

Legacy Software

Unlike data reduction software, legacy software is often an integral part of a new system. Typical legacy systems include software such as:

❑ Financial systems

❑ Database systems

❑ Accounting systems

❏ Order entry systems

❏ Order fulfillment systems

All of these legacy systems must be identified before a test plan is written.

It seems obvious, but do not forget to include the existing software that interfaces with the new system. Be sure that you have the required licenses for the old software if more users will be involved as a direct result of testing. Also, be sure that you are running the correct version of the existing software.

Required Hardware

Next, make sure that you have a handle on all the hardware required for the tests. This list is often much longer than a single line item containing the name of the server on which the new system is running. When considering hardware, think about things such as:

❏ **Communication equipment** — This includes all the items required in the background such as hubs and routers.

❏ **Peripherals** — Be sure to include hardware such as printers.

❏ **Special hardware** — This includes items such as a workstation required for test data generation.

❏ **Facilities** — Be sure to remember any requirements for special test facilities.

When the purpose of a hardware item is not obvious, a brief description of its purpose should be included. This is especially important when independent test groups are responsible for setting up and conducting the tests. It also makes it easy to do a final check that all hardware is in place prior to the commencement of testing activities.

Participating Organizations

Next, list the participating organizations required to conduct the testing, including personnel from the IT department who are required to configure the hardware environment prior to the start of the testing.

Other organizations generally involved in testing include:

❑ **Quality Assurance** — Responsible for witnessing the test and ensuring the accuracy of the results.

❑ **Configuration Management** — Responsible for confirming that the correct version of the software is being tested.

❑ **Management** — Responsible for making a "go or no-go" decision about whether to release the system.

❑ **Development group** — Responsible for providing support to the test group.

❑ **Test group** — Responsible for conducting the test.

For complicated projects, the skill level required of the supporting test personnel should be given some thought and then documented. Include any independent verification personnel, such as the Quality Assurance team that must also be present.

Testing Times

When multiple organizations are involved, which is usually the case when a complex system is tested, it is important to specify the times and dates when personnel from these organizations are required. It is especially important to identify any multi-shift operations required to test a large software program.

Give this some thought. Often, when integrating a new system into an operational data center, off-shift times such as nights are required so as not to interrupt operations any more than necessary. Personnel who typically work the day shift might have to move to nights for a couple of days or weeks when testing takes place. Be sure that you make allowances for this.

All testing activity should be shown on a detailed schedule. Included on the schedule are items such as:

❑ Hardware set up

❑ Dry runs

❑ Runs for record

❑ Data analysis

❑ Final report preparation

The detailed schedule should "tree up" to a line item on the Master Program Schedule. Techniques for developing world-class schedules are covered in Chapter 7, "Scheduling."

Tests To Perform

The next part of the test plan covers testing levels. A test can be conducted at the system level, where there are multiple software entities involved, at the subsystem level, or at the Configuration Item level, where a single software entity is tested.

For each test case, you must also spell out the type of test to be conducted. Examples of test types include:

❑ **Performance testing** — This is where the system is stressed. High load levels are put onto the system to see whether response times are adequate.

❑ **Input/Output testing** — This is where interfaces are tested. Tests can be with other systems or with the end user.

❑ **Functional requirements testing** — This is when all the other "shalls" in the requirements specification are tested. These specifications are the system, subsystem, or Configuration Item requirement specifications.

For each test case, also describe the conditions that apply to the test or group of tests. For example, "Each test shall include nominal, maximum, and minimum values for input data."

Test Results and Analysis

For each test, describe how to record and analyze the test results. Test result recording can be manual or automatic and data reduction can be accomplished via analysis or through data reduction software.

Finally, for each test case include:

❏ **Test objectives** — State the purpose of the test.

❏ **Qualification method** — Specify whether the test is based on analysis, test, demonstration, or inspection.

❏ **Special requirements** — Note any additional steps or conditions needed to conduct the test successfully. For instance, uninterrupted access to a mainframe, or access to special corporate resources, such as existing databases or communication equipment, may be needed. Even access to key personnel might be considered a special requirement.

❏ **Type of data to be recorded** — State what data is required to evaluate how successful the test was. Often a test case generates more data than is required for analysis. This extra data may not be required if it is not specifically needed to validate the requirement to which this test case has been allocated.

❏ **Constraints** — List any restrictions that limit how the test is conducted. For instance, it might be impossible to simulate the actual performance of the system. This might be the result of temporal considerations, such as not being able to run the software for a week at a time or not being able to duplicate the volume of real-life transactions in the test environment.

❏ **Security** — Specify any security requirements imposed by the test.

Test Schedules

A very important section of the test plan is the schedule. Your test schedules should include the following information:

❏ **On-site test periods** — This information describes how long key personnel, hardware, and other resources will be tied up performing the test.

❏ **Estimated time needed for pre-test setup and post-test teardown** — Some testing can be quite involved and require extensive preparation time. This includes system configuration time as well as post-test configuration activities.

❏ **Planned re-testing periods** — Many tests do not run successfully the first time and so regression test time must be planned. Often tests are "dry run" before being "run for record." The term *dry run testing* refers to a test or tests that are run for the sole purpose of ensuring that the test can be completed successfully. Generally, it is an informal test. The term *run for record* refers to a test that is formally witnessed by users or some other organization with the intent of approving the results of the test. Using dry run tests raises the probability of successfully completing the run for record tests.

❏ **Preparation, review, and approval of the test plan** — If senior management or internal procedures require test plan approval before proceeding with testing, then factor the approval time into the overall test cycle. Large corporations may require multiple rewrites of a test plan before approving the final release. Allow plenty of time to get the plan through the required signatures.

Finally, if critical resources, such as mainframes or busy servers are required, the degree of fidelity in the test schedules must be very high.

Requirement Traceability

Finally, all tests should trace to a requirement, and every requirement should have an associated test. Ensuring these two things is the purpose of the requirement traceably section.

Test Procedures

Now that we have covered the details of developing a test plan, let us turn our attention to what goes into a well-written test procedure. For obvious reasons, software should be as bug-free as possible. If for no other reason than self-interest, every developer and IT manager should strive to deliver software that works as advertised. Going back and fixing things is costly and takes time that could be spent on other efforts.

It is generally not possible to test everything, and it is very difficult to deliver a product that is totally bug free unless the system is extremely simple. There are some exceptions. Very small projects can be extensively tested and delivered free of bugs, but more complicated systems always have the potential to be delivered with a few bugs still lurking in all those lines of well-written code.

That said, you as a manager or developer, have to make a decision as to how much testing is enough. To test everything completely on a large system simply might take too long. Some compromises are usually required.

One general guideline is to test the parts of the software that are executed most often. Test those parts thoroughly. Parts of the software that are seldom used can be tested to a lesser extent since the probability of this code causing a bug is less likely.

Another thing to consider is how complicated the code is. Test the most complicated parts hardest since it is there that bugs are most likely to be found.

With those limitations in mind, realize that one key to higher-quality software is to use superior test procedures. True, all software programs require unique test procedures; it is also true that there is no single "cookbook" approach to show you how to write the best procedures. There are, however, guidelines discussed below that will help you produce excellent test procedures. These include guidelines on:

❑ Hardware preparation

❑ Software preparation

❑ Pre-test preparation

❑ Test procedures

❑ Expected results

❑ General requirements

Hardware Preparation

All test procedures should begin with the steps to set up the required hardware configuration. These should be written to such a level that competent technicians not familiar with the project could use them to successfully configure the system. The procedures must cover all hardware connections, including peripherals such as printers.

Use published manuals, such as those provided by hardware manufacturers, when they are available. These manuals often provide the details needed to install the hardware successfully.

For installations that require an extensive hardware suite, the setup procedures should cover:

❑ Specific hardware required to run the test

❑ Specific switch settings or cabling necessary to connect all the hardware items

❑ Diagrams showing the interconnection of the hardware elements

❏ Step-by-step instructions for getting the hardware into the required state for testing

❏ Specification of the storage medium required for the test

For complicated test setups, include a block diagram of the hardware configuration. As mentioned above, this diagram should include all computers, peripheral equipment, and network hardware requirements, such as routers, IP addresses, and connections to legacy hardware required for the tests.

Software Preparation

The next section of a world-class test procedure spells out the details for setting up the required software. This could include databases, operating systems, and the new software.

In the case of commercial software, use published manuals where available. At a minimum, software set-up procedures should include the following information:

❏ Specific software required to run the test

❏ Instructions for loading the software or initializing the software for testing

❏ Instructions for running background support software such as test generators

❏ Procedures for initializing databases and setting up support software such as data collection software and software drivers

Be sure testers are well versed on the operating system of the servers hosting the software.

Pre-Test Preparation

Do not forget to include other pre-test preparation instructions not covered above. These might include limiting access to a server while sensitive performance tests are being run or setting up data capture software. Other items to consider are simulators that must be running during the test or stubbed out software that must be included before testing can begin.

Sometimes testing must be done at a specific time, for instance, on third shift. If this is the case, the test procedure should indicate when it is possible to begin testing.

Test Procedures

All test procedures should begin with a brief description of the purpose of the test. Describe what the test should accomplish, how long the test should take, and any specific information test personnel need to be aware of before the test is started.

Next, the actual test procedures should be listed. Test procedures are specific steps a tester is required to take in order to execute the test. Specific things to include are:

❏ Procedures to set flags, breakpoints, data, or control parameters

❏ Procedures to set initial conditions

❏ Procedures for each step of the test

❏ Special procedures such as those required to modify databases

❏ Procedures to repeat a test case, if necessary

❏ Procedures to stop the test, if required, and to record data or make measurements

❏ Procedures to resume a suspended test

❏ Procedures to analyze test results

If special input data is required for a procedure, then it also needs to be specified. For each input, the following information is helpful:

❏ Name, purpose, and description (e.g., range of values, accuracy) of the test input

❏ Source of the test input and the method used for selecting the test input

❏ Whether the test input is real or simulated

❏ Type of test input (e.g., worst case, out of bounds data, normal data, etc.)

Writing good test procedures is difficult. It will often be discovered that the test procedure is not adequate once the testing begins. One way to improve the overall quality of test procedures is to dry run them before real testing takes place. Often, this technique will greatly improve the test procedures, making the real test proceed much more smoothly.

Another good idea is to evaluate each test procedure prior to testing. As a general rule, the more eyes seeing and commenting on the procedure, the better. This improves test procedure quality significantly.

Expected Results

The next section, one of the most important, is the expected results for each test. In many cases, the correct result of a test can have a fairly large range of acceptable values. With that point in mind, each set of expected results should also specify the criteria for determining success. Some general guidelines are:

❏ Specify the range or accuracy over which the output is acceptable.

❏ Specify conditions under which the results are inconclusive.

❏ Specify conditions indicating anomalies.

❏ Specify the location of expected results. For example, specify the file and directory where test results will be stored.

❏ Specify name and usage instructions for data reduction software required to analyze large data files.

In the case where multiple results can be expected, each result should be covered.

General Requirements

There are other items to consider when preparing a test procedure. These are listed below.

Requirements Traceability

All test cases must trace directly to one or more requirements. These can be software requirements as specified in a Software Requirements Specification, subsystem requirements, or system requirements as specified in the associated requirements specifications. When a test case covers more than one requirement, the procedures for the test case should be correlated with all requirements being tested.

Constraints

Many times a test is just that, a test. It is often impossible, in a test environment, to mimic real-world operations. In these cases, constraints imposed on the test procedure should be documented. This might include throughput limitations or data limitations.

In the event that there are constraints, these constraints must correlate with some sort of success criteria. For example, on a performance test where throughput is constrained, an analysis might be conducted showing that if a certain volume of transactions were achieved during the test, then based on some type of analysis, it can be extrapolated that the volume will scale up to the volume expected on the production system.

Notes

This section contains any general information that aids in understanding the test. The notes section is also a good place to put an acronym list and any abbreviations used in the test procedures.

Writing good test procedures takes time, but the results are well worth the effort.

Glossary

ACWP: Actual Cost of Work Performed

BAC: Budget at Completion

BCWP: Budgeted Cost of Work Performed

BCWS: Budgeted Cost of Work Scheduled

CI: Configuration Item

CM: Configuration Management

CSCS: Cost and Schedule Control System

EAC: Estimate at Completion

HCI: Hardware Configuration Item

HUL: Hardware Utilization List

QA: Quality Assurance

ROI: Return on Investment

SOW: Statement of Work

SRS: System Requirements Specification

TBD: To Be Determined

TRS: Technical Requirements Specification

Index

C